LAMENTATION OF A SOUL

LAMENTATION OF A SOUL

by Hope Agu (little Mary of the Most Sacred Heart of Jesus)

Bibliographical Information of the Deutsche Nationalbibliothek
This publication is listed in the Deutsche Nationalbibliographie of the Deutsche Nationalbibliothek; detailed bibliographical information can be accessed under http: //dnb.d-nb.de

© 2016 Hope Agu – little Mary of the Most Sacred Heart of Jesus
Printing, Production and Layout: BoD – Books on Demand, Norderstedt
ISBN: 978-3-7431-2979-5

Contents

PREFACE	7
CHAPTER I AGONIZED HEART	9
CHAPTER II THE INCARNATION	19
CHAPTER III MORE VALUE THAN THE SPARROWS	28
CHAPTER IV THE BODY OF CHRIST	41
CHAPTER V POLITICAL DECAY	66
CHAPTER VI LITTLE SOULS	85
CHAPTER VII THE EUCHARIST	99
CHAPTER VIII SELF ESTEEM	114
CHAPTER IX COMPLETE DELIVERANCE	122

CHAPTER X TOTAL SURRENDER TO GOD'S LOVE	137
CHAPTER XI MARY MY MUM	147
CHAPTER XII THE PRIEST	161
CHAPTER XIII AWARENESS	170
CHAPTER XIV INGRATITUDE	180
CHAPTER XV THE BEAUTY OF MOTHERHOOD	189
CHAPTER XVI INTERFERENCE	195
CHAPTER XVII CONCLUSION	204

PREFACE

To be able to assess the depth of pain experienced in the heart due to unrequited love, one must first be privileged to feel love for someone who does not take notice of his or her existence, or a married man or woman dumped by the partner for someone else, especially when that someone else is far below his or her caliber. Should one not be privileged to be in such a situation then one can make do with the vacuum in the heart at the loss of a close friend or relative. Unrequited love is the most heart rending pain, therefore, with this on mind, one can have a slight glimpse, though it be beyond human imagination, of the depth of the agony in the Heart of the God who created us, whose children we are, when we reject His Love which He so generously gives us freely. Most parents would, I presume, understand, due to the pain they experience, when their children reject their love, as a result of misconception of their parental responsibilities with regards to the method of their upbringing, resulting to their children keeping their distance, when they leave home and get into professional life, married or otherwise, making no attempt to keep in touch with them, their parents. For such children the word 'parent' becomes a vocabulary. Surely this attitude is very heart-rending to any unfortunate parent. On the other hand, children whose most concern are their God-given parents, happen to be those who experienced a wealth of happy childhood. These children, in their adulthood, cherish the parents who raised them up, who guided their steps as they grew into maturity until they became independent therefore, in gratitude for the love received during childhood, shower their parents with so much love and affection. Such children are very dear to their parents who in turn willingly grant them their blessing. They are the pride of their parents who are pleased their efforts were not in vain. God is not different. He is a FATHER, our Father. The Father of all humanity to

Whom we owe love, obedience, subordination and loyalty. A fact to be acknowledged by all as we owe Him our existence and all that we are. It would be wrong to reject God, the Destiny of humanity. Denial of His existence and His rejection ends up in the ultimate consequence, damnation.

Awake O man and hearken to the voice of your Father who is in Heaven. Is there something He has not done to prove His Love for you? Is the sacrifice of His only begotten Son not enough for you? Can you be able to imagine the depth of the mental and physical torture your God endured for you? Do you realize the risk He took in His Incarnation for your salvation, to restore to you the glory that was yours from the beginning? To restore the paradise lost with the fall of Adam and Eve? Why not relax in the imagination of your mind and grant yourself the luxury of visualizing the paradise, free from any kind of ailment, rich in love, tranquility and equilibrium, lacking nothing. What a contrast to the world of today. That notwithstanding, anything could have happened to our Beloved Savior, to Jesus Christ, the only begotten Son of the Father, for the risk He took in His Incarnation, considering the danger He confronted which threatened His life from the moment of His conception, but your comfort, your salvation, your eternal joy with Him in Heaven was His priority, therefore, He chose to suffer and hung for three agonizing painful hours on the cross under the weight of His body, a bitter shameful death for love of humanity. Be the child (children) He created you to be and comfort your Father who is in Heaven by returning love for love. Love your God, He deserves it.

CHAPTER I

AGONIZED HEART

In retrospection, I was very much impressed, when I realized how much I resemble God, the Almighty Father without knowing I did. It was then it occurred to me the reason I possess the nature that I have which was prominent while I was at school. How amazing it is we are in God and yet live out of God, taking things for granted for the simple reason we do not give enough thought to what is going on in us and around us. The puzzle about us would have been solved long before we knew it had we obliged ourselves with self-scrutiny. It would have enabled us find ourselves closer to God than we thought, consequently saving us the problem of the after effect of estrangement from the wonderful good God humanity has as Father. Jesus Glorious Reign of Peace would have come.

Somehow, right from childhood, I have had the inclination of showing mercy which I inherited from my biological parents, I presume, who would never hesitate to give a helping hand to anyone in need. My mother once said she would rather prefer her children in tattered clothes than have someone who lives with her and serves her, in tattered clothes. The doors of my parental home were always opened for the poor. As children we were privileged to observe the joy they derived in doing good which left a great imprint in us helping to form our respective character.

As a teenager, during my secondary school years, in St. Catherine's girls secondary school Nkwere in Nigeria, a boarding school, being a peace loving girl, I found it difficult to express anger for long to the joy of my mates. Nwando Iweka, the daughter of a medical doctor who became a girl-friend of mine in elementary school, as events would have it, we were privileged to enter the same secondary school, took advantage of my peaceful disposition. Whenever she herself or someone else offended me all that was needed to bring me laughing out loud, a hearty laughter, by which I was known, was simply a smile. A simple smile from my offender generated such laughter that spoke my vacant mind causing the anger to subside, the offender forgiven regardless what the offence was. Unfortunately, in the course of events in my life this hearty- laughter was lost until Jesus restored it in a more beautiful and meaningful manner. To be merciful and forgiving, and having love for my neighbor has been part of me. Had I been able to relate these virtues to God and realized He infused them in me I would not have gone through so many waters as I did in my poor miserable life. A thorough examination of self helps reveal to man his resemblance to God from whom he came, his Creator, the heavenly Father of humanity. Then would man be able to realize, in his scrutiny of self, that even the little glimpse of goodness in him is from God, for every child resembles, in one way or the other, his parent. Therefore, if one nourishes that little glimpse of goodness in one, the sign he is part of God who is Goodness, it will make him docile and reciprocal to Providence, to Divine Love which God the Father is continually offering. How sad it is the failure of humanity to detect God in himself and accept Divine Assistance to the Glory of God.

Tears, o tears, my sweet companion dear,
Sweet longing, o companion most dear,
Hopeful expectation, my Beloved most dear,
Whose Arms consolation sweet embrace be,
For troubled nerves sweet tonic provides.

Tears o tears, my sweet companion dear,
Desire, passion, o delightful sweet longing,
Expectations, sweet delight of hope so sweet

From a Beloved most dear. Something seems
nothing, for Love so sweet so pure so Holy.

O dreams, sweet beautiful unfulfilled dreams
of yesterday, joyfully today come sweetly alive.
Lovingly awakened by Jesus, Bridegroom most
Sweet. His Sweetness and Beauty only lovers
know. The union of hearts in passionate bliss.

And yet why is my heart troubled, why this sadness lingering in my heart amidst Heaven in this thorny exile. To comprehend my state there is the necessity for an objective examination of conscience with the aim to understand the God of creation who has been in agony ever since He created man. Having endowed man with perfection, enriched him with Virtues, Graces, and infinite Love, He reaped, as reward, ingratitude, disappointment, betrayal, lack of trust, unfaithfulness from the man in whom He has delight to have created.

Out of a vast emptiness, nothing existed, but God, who was content and at peace with Himself, in His Triune Self, lacking nothing simply being Himself – LOVE. Out of the abundance of His goodness, He began to create, having so much love, Beauty and wealth to lavish. The pleasure in His Creation induced Him to create man after His own image, the perfection of His creation, to enjoy all that He created. This gave rise to His nightmare from which He is yet to recover. His peaceful existence was disrupted, paving way to the most bitter sacrifice a God of love would make in the course of realizing His Vision.

Unto what should it be likened, unto a young man who, having climbed the peak of his professional ladder, feeling financially stable and content, he decides to settle down into a family life, as he is now in the position to maintain wife and children and lavish his hard earned money on them.

So it was also with God who has so much love and wealth to lavish. Alas! man, who is His Kingdom, who is to share His Divine Life with Him, failed Him woefully, betrayed Him without remorse. At the slightest trial, a proof of loyalty and love, man failed woefully by yielding to the temptation of the serpent, Lucifer the devil, a replica of ingratitude and greed, who in his wicked desire to be god deceived man to distrust God.

Nevertheless, God in His Infinite Mercy and Goodness still loves the man He created with infinite love. Therefore, man being part of God Who is madly in love with him, has his ultimate destiny in God, without Whom man has no peace. As a child resembles the parent, God Who is Love, being the Father of humanity, the human nature is also love, God's Love. The human nature is God's nature and only God, through His Grace, can restore pure Love, true Love, Holy Love in man, as man in his sinful nature came short of this Love and indulges in lust, sinful love which offends God. Therefore, God desires to transform humanity by feeding him with Himself to enable him live with Him in Heaven if man allows Him.

> When Belief, Hope, Trust, in One Most Faithful,
> Most Loving, Most Sweet, sweet Companion be
> Born is Humility, Virtue Most Divine, Most noble,
> Most sweet, precious Key to Heavenly Bliss,
> Eternal Delight in the Arms of Beloved so Sweet.
>
> O little me, less than half of an Ant you be,
> How overwhelmed you must be, His Majesty,
> King of Glory, on you His Love doth so lavish.
> O wretched creature, wisdom is spelt in gratitude,
> A noble garment, for Love so Divine, in which you
> are so beautifully clothed by Beloved so Divine.

Man's betrayal was a slap on God's face. Consequent to this betrayal sin entered man causing a demarcation between Him and God. He is thrown out of the garden of Eden, striped of his immortality and friendship with God. God hates sin like the pest, yet His nature being Love, having created man and placed so much attachment on him, so much love, He yearns for the love of man which is His Divine Right. God, the Alpha and Omega, created for His own pleasure. In His Infinite Goodness and Mercy, He created man for Himself, for Love. It is indeed very astonishing to observe that neither Eve nor Adam repented their error, rather they had only excuses for God for the pain in His Heart due to their betrayal, fully aware of His Love for them. Eve's excuse "the serpent beguiled me and I did eat" and Adam's "the woman you gave me..." portray the depth to which they fell. They failed to realize the depth of sorrow they caused such a generous God who created them and adorned them with so much love and goodness. In their betrayal, which generated pride, an undesirable attribute, they became blind, so much so, they became unable to utter the beautiful word "sorry" which is the simple means of appeasing and consoling such a loving and most merciful God who would not have hesitated to show them mercy. Events would have taken a different turn. However, having made themselves docile to the serpent, Satan or devil, the embodiment of ingratitude, greed, selfishness, pride, and arrogance, Adam and Eve paved way for sin, the ultimate loss of friendship with God and the paradise where they were so much sheltered and showered with love and affection, thereby leaving an awful testament, mortality, the result of sin, a terrible inheritance, for all their children from generation to generation.

Nevertheless, God could not detach Himself from man forever therefore, unable to bear the suffering His beloved children were undergoing, due to the influence of sin, He chose to mold a nation, Israel, after His own heart, as model, for keeping His precepts from which others would learn. For this purpose, Abraham was chosen, through him God intended to bless the world, a covenant was established. The nation Israel was born from the seeds of Jacob, Esau was his elder brother, son of Isaac the son of Abraham. Unfortunately, this nation, in turn, became a thorn in the Flesh for God. The children of Israel, became with their unfaithfulness, a failure, killing the prophets sent to them and worshiped strange gods much to the displeasure of the Almighty God. How easily did they forget the great deeds of God, how he led them with a mighty hand out of the Land of Egypt where they were in perpetual slavery, the victory He gave them in the different wars He fought for them. Although God punished them for their errors, after a long rope of unfruitful warning, God Himself suffered more than the children He punished because He is LOVE! A very loving Father perfect in His judgement. He cannot be less than He is. "Woe is me because of my hurt! my wound is grievous. But I said, "Truly this is my affliction and I must bear it" The Father's pain over the pending exile of the children of Israel due to their constant disobedience to His Holy Will. "...How often would I have gathered your children together as a hen gathers her brood under her wings, and you would not" Jesus over Jerusalem. A heart-rending cry of unrequited love from a God of Love. How my heart aches for the sorrows of my God.

God has been in agony ever since the fall of man and my heart laments over the hardness of man and his deafness to the appeal of God the Father who is madly in love with him appealing to him to return. A most loving Father who has thrown open the ocean of His Divine Mercy, pleading for its acceptance, a further attempt to protect His Beloved from the impending and inevitable perdition if His plea is ignored.

> O Love, sweet beautiful Love of Father so Divine,
> Rich in Mercy, Compassion, Goodness, Tolerance,
> Understanding, kindness, Patience, Generosity, O
> and so much more such sweet Virtues that flow
> abundantly never ending, greater than the ocean, far
> beyond the human imagination in every dimension.
> It's Love Divine, the Heavenly Father's Love.

What a wonderful Dad You are Father Most Divine.
From Your Throne in Heaven, Your Child here Below,
With loving watchful Eyes You Behold, from every
Danger protect, with loving fatherly care Graces You
bestow, O loving Graces, the Father's Love display,
In deep appreciation, the child lost in admiration of
the Dad so wonderful, the Father Most Divine.

O how sweet Love sounds, the Name of Father so Divine,
Pure, beautiful, sweet Love, of the Father so Divine. His only
begotten Son, for the child beloved, He did not spare. How
wonderful the Father's Love be for His child, His little girl. O
how awesome! In Heaven He be, here below in His Divine
Son in the Host He be, a Prisoner of Love, day and night
for His child, His little girl. O how sweet, how beautiful, how
wonderful, is the tender loving care of Father so Divine.

The Creation portrays the Father's handwriting of love. The beautifully created Universe with all its natural sceneries, the great abundance of nourishment in different assortments, on land and in the sea, to the taste of every individual, the natural resources, should send the signal to everyone, God of Creation is a loving Father. However, the indifferences, the coldness, ingratitude dished out to Him daily is most unfair. How could arrogance, flamboyantly displayed, without remorse, rob a level-headed person the capability to realize the danger in rejecting God's Love. How could one be thoughtless of the injury inflicted to the Heart of God, our Father, who loves humanity with such infinite love, who is waiting patiently, drawing attention to His burning desire for an intimate relationship with humanity, to give them Heaven. Why should one lock up the heart when Jesus our Lord, our Most merciful Savior stands and knocks? Why reject God? When will man awake from slumber, ponder on the God of Creation who fills the universe with goodness and keep His precepts, return love for Love, bearing on mind everyone is keeping time in preparation for the final abode when the departing bell is sounded. Therefore, make hay while the sun shines, seek the Creator, God the Father while He can be found and pass through His merciful Heart which is open to all, even to the worst sinner. Be wise and make a U – Turn back into the Arms of the Heavenly Father who loves you infinitely and cease from hurting Him. All there is to it is simply a repentant heart and the penitent will find peace and come to the possession of his heart's desire.

Perhaps, it sounds amazing, incomprehensible that the Almighty God, Creator of Heaven and earth, Author and Giver of Life, without whom nothing exists, The Supreme Being, is agonized. How is it possible a self-content triune God is agonized? Agony, what is it? Great pain or suffering of the mind or body. Yes, the Almighty God is self-content, but He is Love and Father. He is the Father of mankind, the children He created in His likeness and fell madly in love with. He wants to give them Heaven, He wants them to have Life. They should live with Him in Him and for Him eternally. He does not want to lose any of them to perdition. The Almighty God has for humanity a motherly love. His protective nature coupled with His desire for their safety in His warm Embrace subject Him to agony due to the lack of trust and unrequited love from them. Jesus Christ, the Beloved Redeemer, is in dire agony as a great number of His Children are not paying heed to all His warnings against the wickedness being webbed by Satan, whose ultimate end is perdition, who, aware of his woeful end, craftily seduces and entices the weak minded who are blinded with the riches and pomp of this terrible world of transient. In his insatiable desire for company in hell, though mostly to hurt God, Satan manipulates the human mind against God, aware of God's attachment to humanity. Everyone should realize that to hurt God is to hurt one self, therefore Satan is not only using man to hurt God he uses man to hurt man for God is man's Destiny, man's Eternal joy.

Nevertheless, one may dare ask, since God cares so much for all His children why not have every one saved and spare Himself the trouble of the agony. A very good and logical question indeed, but one should not forget God's nature is Love and Love does not compel therefore, God who is Love endowed every individual with a free-will. Besides God cannot be less than He is. It is entirely an individual opinion the choice he makes, either to be on God's side and choose Eternal Life or on Satan's side and choose Eternal Death. Jesus Christ, with His bitter Passion brought Redemption to the entire human race, thus reconciled humanity with God, His Most Precious Blood being the Price. What a wonderful Father God is. For the security of His Children He took Flesh, conquered death for them, defeated the powers of darkness, triumphed with His resurrection and opened the gate of Heaven for them. God the Father is indeed the best Dad. He risked His priceless possession, the life and security of His only begotten Son by sending Him into our filthy world, amidst His enemies, to become one of us, clothed with poverty, He tasted every aspect of human suffering, became sin so that we may have life. Jesus emptied Himself in His passion, a most terribly, horrifying passion, the hour of darkness in which Satan mobilized His children against Him, whereby they gave their Father the worst torture never before heard of nor ever would be heard of again. The human mind will never be able to comprehend all that Jesus had to bear physically and mentally. It was far more than is ever revealed. His capability to withstand that test was Love from which He drew strength, courage and the Will to fulfill the Father's Will otherwise, He would not have made it in His humanity. It was an excessively too great a torture for anyone to bear considering the long duration. However, the love for the Father, to bring back to Him what was lost, the love for humanity, to save the world, gave Him strength, courage, the Will to persevere until finally He made it. "Father into thy Hand I commend my Spirit" "It is finished" Love triumphed over wickedness. Good defeated evil. The powers of darkness disappointed. The cross victorious.

Therefore, should anyone land in Hell, whether the existence of Hell is believed in or not, is entirely one's own responsibility. Hell is real just as Heaven is real. Jesus the Way, the Truth and The Life acknowledged the existence of hell, so not to believe in hell is total blindness and unwise. Anyone who does not believe in hell will definitely be compelled to do so when he eventually lands there. Bear on mind, hell has only a one-way ticket, there is no return ticket. Whoever lands there should have himself entirely to blame because Jesus gives everyone enough opportunity for a change of heart, to denounce evil and choose the Good by keeping His commandments and abiding in His Love. God should not be blamed hence He has done everything to prove His Divine Love for His wayward and blind children who have refused to see the agony in the Heart of their God pleading for them to return love for love for their own benefits. Despite that He continues His never wavering effort in sounding a loving bell of warning for His children to choose life, bear their respective crosses in charity, obedience and humility, loving one another as He has loved them, following His example as this is the only way to reach the promised land. The Almighty God, is knocking, like a beggar, on every heart, so let everyone clothe himself with wisdom, trust in Jesus, while one can, let the door of hearts open, and may the ocean of God's Divine Mercy be appreciated before He comes as a just judge, so as to have life more abundantly in God's Glory and avoid the inevitable perdition.

Is it not wonderful, good and beautiful the knowledge man proceeded from God and will eventually go back to Him? A wonderful knowledge indeed, the awareness one originated from God, the Father of the human race, it intoxicates with happiness and delight, so man has identity after all. This realization, however, gives the hardships of this planet Earth a new and worthy meaning, as the ultimate goal for man is Heaven, the Eternal abode of God the Father, confirming transient as the inevitable fate of the planet Earth making nothing to be but what is not.

CHAPTER II

THE INCARNATION

If there was anything so beautiful, so awesome, so marvelous, so miraculous and so Divine, it was the Word made Flesh. The second Person of the Trinity became man! How was it that the invisible God of the old Israel, I AM, the Almighty God, decided to make Himself known to humanity in the third Person of the Holy Trinity, in Jesus Christ? Was it simply the urge to redeem humanity? What exactly prompted this Divine gesture?

Oh, it's wonderful to realize it was His fatherly instinct, instigated by Love – Divine Love – selfless love for the Beloved. Such love does not count the cost. All that matters is the well-being of the Beloved to the point of emptying oneself, suffering to the bitter end. God is, in the first place Father. He loves being a Father and He dotes on the children He created therefore, He would go to any length for their safety. "I have delight in the human race" this way God revealed His infinite attachment to humanity.

As revealed in the Holy Scripture, the fall of man was instigated by Satan due to greed, pride and disobedience. Now having misled Adam and Eve through whom sin penetrated into the world, the garden of Eden turned into a pungent smell, from sin, much to the displeasure of God. This awful result of disobedience, which in itself destroyed the paradise on earth, designed with the finger of God, wherewith His infinite Love for man was portrayed, created a rift between God and man. That notwithstanding, had Adam and Eve been penitent, God would have forgiven them being such a sweet good God and bountiful in

Mercy. It is most astonishing that Lucifer, the Satan, having tasted God's goodness and favor, turned evil, blinded with pride, in his meanness, fully aware of the consequences of his evil intentions, dared interfere in the affairs of God Who is his Benefactor, the God to whom he owes his existence, the God who loved him. His self-willed, mischievous evil act, the seduction of Adam and Eve to betray God's trust and friendship, which in his vanity he took for triumph, consequently generated enmity between him and the most compassionate, Good and Merciful God whose name is LOVE. There might have been the possibility for sin to be reversed while at its bud, preventing it from infiltrating into generations upon generations of the human race if events had taken a different turn, whereby the plain-tiffs, Adam and Eve, accepted their wrong-doing and uttered the simple word "sorry" which would have resulted in the Incarnation being unnecessary thereby saving God so much trouble. Should it on the long run be His Divine Will to make Himself physically known He would then, in His infinite Wisdom, have chosen a more convenient means than the hazardous and terrible bitter way of His passion. Nevertheless, despite all odds, the All Knowing and Ever Loving Protective Heavenly Father could not have had a better design for the redemption of the human race, providing her with the loveliest, beautiful, clement and sweet, Mother that ever was, ever is and ever will be, Immaculately conceived, the masterpiece of God. A genuinely remarkable Divine gesture, portraying the generosity of the God of Mercy, which surpasses, in great measure, the Divine Vision for humanity in the garden of Eden, whereby humanity was merely a friend, whereas in the new Vision humanity becomes, not only a friend, but also adopted into the Family of God and heir with His Only Begotten Son, Our Lord Jesus Christ, as His mother becomes the mother of the human race. What a marvelous inheritance! Humanity is most blessed, a reason to be most grateful to God and turn the back to Satan.

However, having chewed His disappointment, when nothing else could atone for sin, the sacrifice of a young and spotless lamb, as the chosen people, the old Israel, repeatedly fell woefully back into sin, God sent His Only Begotten Son into the world to serve the purpose. "for God so loved the world that he gave his only son, that whoever believes in him should not perish but have eternal life" Thus fulfilling the prophesy of Isaiah "a young woman shall conceive and bear a son, and shall call his name Immanuel" which John in his Gospel consequently confirmed. "And the word became flesh and dwelt among us, full of grace and truth; we beheld his glory, the glory as of the only son from the Father"

God's protective nature for His beloved children instigated Him to take flesh in order to bridge the gap created by sin between Him and the human race. Having created them in His own Image He took delight in them and gave them His Heart. This sweet gesture of God created in Him a feeling of incompleteness without the human race as He conferred to them the identity of being His children. Having done so He dotes on them and desires to shower them with Love. He yearns for the reunion with His children for them to share His glory with Him, to spend Eternal Life with Him in His Divinity. As a result, God whose nature is Love desires to see Love in humanity, a reflection of Himself. Therefore, Human beings should be Love to resemble their Heavenly Father Whose nature is Love. Unfortunately, God's failure to see His Reflection in humanity sends His Sacred Heart into Agony. Therefore, this Agony of our Lord Jesus Christ, lies within the hand of humanity to turn it into delight.

What a bitter struggle between Good and evil! God who infinitely loves the human race with a motherly love, has been struggling to save His children from the destructive power of Satan, the evil one, whose sole aim is to destroy God's children, the human race, with his wickedness, due to his perpetual malignity, in order to bring God into contempt. The Eternal Father, Author and giver of life, infinite Goodness, the Almighty God, in His loving concern for the fate of His beloved children and this terrible world, sent Him, the second person of the Holy Trinity, Jesus

Christ, begotten of the Father not made, one with the Father, from His Heavenly Throne into this filthy world, into the world He created, polluted by Satan and his subordinates, for the salvation of His children which He alone, as the innocent Lamb of God, can accomplish.

God in His motherly nature for His children would do anything for their happiness, according to His nature, Love. This ultimately gave rise to the bitter passion of our Lord Jesus Christ. It is most remarkably admirable, utterly praiseworthy, this Divine gesture of God, to sacrifice His only begotten Son for the salvation of humanity, a confirmation of the acknowledgement, God would stop at nothing for the happiness of humanity, the crown of His creation, as long as it is beneficial to souls in His perspective, being the Alpha and Omega who cannot change. This exceptionally unique sacrifice in the total surrender of the Son to the Father's Will in complete emptying of self-unto death, though aware Satan was to mobilize His Beloved children against Him, instigate them to serve Him the most terrible painful torture never before heard of in history, in his evil and greedy intention to possess the world he did not create, is highly praiseworthy. This heroic and loving gesture of our Lord Jesus Christ has worn for Him, from the human race, an unending gratitude in eternal adoration and worship. The omniscient God, aware of Satan's wicked signature in the abomination of His children committed against Him, their Father, chained and imprisoned, pulled like a beast of burden, the terrible disgrace of His stripping, mockery, scourging, crowing with thorns, the strenuous burden of the cross, spilling of His Most Precious Blood on the streets of Jerusalem, the stretching of His Limbs, dislocating them as they nailed Him on the cross, bearing on mind also the awful agony in the garden of Gethsemane, such terribly frightening mental torture He experienced, portrayed in the sweating of His Divine Blood, oh, and so many more not revealed, finally the humiliating death on the cross, yet He succumbed to it all for their redemption. Despite all that was done to Him He forgave them all. He paid the depth for sin. Forgiveness therefore, becomes an indispensable virtue for every soul in the pursuit of Divine Grace. Reciprocation to God's love is inevitable to achieve victory over man's arch enemy, Satan, for Eternal Salvation.

"Hail Mary full of grace" the greeting of St. Gabriel, the Archangel to the Blessed Virgin Mary at the annunciation to receive the beautiful, famous, victorious, most admirable word "Yes" that most consoled the Heart of God. Thereafter, the Word became Flesh in her womb which in turn became the first human Tabernacle of the triune God. Now if the Almighty God, the immortal and invincible God has such confidence in humanity, trusting Himself entirely to Joseph and Mary to enable Him bring salvation to humanity, why then is it a problem for humanity to give Him their trust. If He, the Creator, fully aware of the risks involved yet ventured to dive into it, what then could have been the driving factor if not love. A God who loves His creatures so much as to risk everything for love of them, surely must have their interest at Heart. It is, therefore, most amazing the indifferences, lack of trust and the nonchalant attitude with which the Almighty God, Father and Creator of humanity is being treated by His creatures. How wonderfully amazing it is pondering on the fact the Almighty God was a tiny ovary in the womb for nine months, became vulnerable, learnt to crawl, sit and walk like every normal child, dependent on His parents, worked obediently as a Help to His Foster Father, Joseph, in his carpentry work. It is interesting to visualize Him, God, working as an obedient and subordinate son in the work shop. The thought He walked on this filthy world, breathing the same air should indeed provide food for thought for every individual. As it is rightly said, there is no smoke without fire, therefore, the Almighty God, in His infinite Wisdom, must have seen it as the means suitable for the salvation of mankind, a fact which no one should ignore or take for granted, but rather contemplate with humility and awe the mystery and greatness of the Almighty God.

Jesus Christ, who being God, dwelt among us as the only begotten of the Father, spent three good years of His thirty-three years on earth to teach and call to the human mind the awareness of the precepts of God, to find that which was lost and God's desire to be loved as Father. Although a very trying and strenuous three years, as He was confronted with much opposition from the Pharisees and publicans, yet, as one with authority He imparted to humanity the meaning of life and disclosed the identity of the human race with compassion proclaiming the coming of the Kingdom of God, the need for repentance, to store up treasures in Heaven rather than trusting in the perishable wealth of this world.

Instigated by Love, being Love, an assignment from the Father which He dutifully, patiently and with genuine compassion fulfilled with perfection. It is not to be forgotten, although being fully Divine He was also fully human and exposed to every temptation to which every human being is prone to encounter on his pilgrimage in this terrifying wilderness, the exile world. Being truly human one cannot help but admire the brilliant manner with which Jesus overcame the temptations of the devil who, in his craftiness, tempting Him at the time he thought he would easily achieve his purpose, Jesus having fasted for forty days in the wilderness after His baptism. The excellent performance of Jesus in overcoming the temptations demonstrates the ability of humanity to overcome sin, if sincere efforts are made trusting in God for Grace, Jesus having redeemed the human race with His Precious Blood. So to that end, with the focus on Jesus the Redeemer, who never left His focus on the Father, everyone is capable of excelling brilliantly from sin to the displeasure of Satan, the wicked devil and to the pleasure of God, our Heavenly Father.

How could an Omniscient God permit evil to exist if He loved humanity He created with infinite love? What a burdensome, dominating question that often permeates the mind, especially depraved minds, with a devastating consequence, throwing one into the state of unbelief in the existence of God. To those battling with such questions, God does not permit evil to exist rather He sent His only begotten Son, Jesus Christ into the world, not for pleasure, but for the redemption of the world in order to put an end to evil. Although Satan is the originator of evil, as his name defines, humanity gives him a helping hand when they indulge in greed, self-esteem, pride, covetousness, envy, bribery and corruption, consequently becoming docile for the influence of Satan and cease to abide in God's Love. Do not be deceived, God is a God of love and He detests evil. All God has been trying to do is to convince man of His love and save him from his ultimate damnation, if he fails to reciprocate His love and accept His outstretched Arm of Divine Mercy, he should not blame God. There is no use for logic in the acknowledgement of God's goodness and mercy, all there is to it is a simple surrender to the Author and Giver of life, the Almighty God who created the universe and the Heavens. With the total sacrifice of His only Son who emptied Himself completely for the redemption of humanity, the Almighty God has proved with perfection His good intentions, His love for humanity. Jesus Christ conquered the powers of darkness with His victorious cross, His glorious Resurrection, the triumph over death, guarantees Eternal Life for everyone who humbly acknowledges and accepts it in gratitude. Evil is not of God but of Satan. God is Love. He does not compel anyone to believe in Him, although His Heart aches and longs that everyone would, but He cannot be less than He is. In His infinite love for humanity He gave free-will to all. Nevertheless, Satan has been driven out from Heaven into the bottomless pit from where he wonders about deceiving God's children and turning them against Him. There he awaits the final judgement when evil ceases, and Satan and his subordinates finally end up in perdition. What a time to look forward to, a time to be with the Lord Jesus Christ eternally in Heaven.

However, sin having polluted humanity due to the interference of Satan in the lives of Adam and Eve, humanities first parents, sin must be burned out of man to enable man attain the glory destined for Him by God from the beginning. Man's destiny is eternal life with God in Jesus Christ, for Him, with Him and in Him. For the realization of this beautiful heavenly destiny is to take up ones cross and follow Christ. As Jesus rightly put it, the way to damnation is broad, but that of eternal life is narrow and few there be that find it. This is because so many people get themselves entangled with the riches and pomp of this sinful world contaminated by Satan. Nevertheless, Jesus the Beloved Savior is the answer to all the puzzling questions of this confused world. If there was nothing in it after all, why should the only Son of the highest God undergo such terrible bodily and mental torture in the name of redeeming mankind. There is a saying of the Nigerian Ibos, "Awo ada agba oso efife na nkiti" meaning literary, a frog does not run for nothing in the afternoon – there is no smoke without fire. Therefore, the wisest thing is to hearken to the appeal of Jesus Christ who desires every single soul to be saved, bear your cross together with Jesus. To dare to bear it alone spells failure. He is ever ready to assist. There is no other way to the promised land. All ailment which befalls humanity, the good Lord Jesus has experienced in a most bitter form on His blessed body. Satan is the cause of evil not the good loving and merciful God.

Do not therefore, be frightened with the natural catastrophes happening in our time. Be rest assured everything happens out of love. Do you realize God is most affected by it all due to the pains they cause His beloved children? You weep and are in sorrow for the loss of a loved one, whose fate is justly taken care of by our righteous Father, whereby your Beloved Heavenly Father weeps and is in sorrow for the pain in your own heart for your loss. Oh, how happy He would be if He had no cause for such natural catastrophies. He is Almighty, all Powerful, surely He is not expected to sound a warning with a simple stick. Who would notice. A father chastises whom he loves. If one spares the rod one spoils the child. Besides, God prefers not to chastise than to chastise as He feels the pain more than the children He chastises. It is sad most people do not realize this. The natural catastrophies would not be if humanity would learn from it and pay heed to the commandments of God. The problem is, rather than learn and realize God is sending out warnings to sound His existence by exhibiting His power, out of love, for a change of heart, on our part, how we treat Him, we fall back to the old practices as soon as everything dies down. He is still trying to assist the children for whom He shed His most precious Blood reach the promised land. If only everyone would realize this world is transitory and would be destroyed by fire, seek the everlasting habitation in Heaven with Jesus in joy eternal, detach oneself from the perishable wealth of this sick world, from sexual laxity, maintain natural laws as God desires, then Satan would be put to book, consequently, ushering Christ's glorious reign of peace.

CHAPTER III

MORE VALUE THAN THE SPARROWS

"Therefore I tell you, do not be anxious about your life, what you shall eat, nor about your body, what you shall put on. For life is more than food, and the body more than clothing. Consider the ravens: they neither sow nor reap, they have neither storehouse nor barn, and yet God feeds them. Of how much more value are you than the birds! And which of you by being anxious can add a cubit to his span of life? If then you are not able to do as small a thing as that, why are you anxious about the rest? Consider the lilies, how they grow; they neither toil nor spin; yet I tell you, even Solomon in all his glory was not arrayed like one of these. But if God so clothes the grass which is alive in the field today and tomorrow is thrown into the oven, how much more will he clothe you, O men of little faith! And do not seek what you are to eat and what you are to drink, nor be of anxious mind. For all the nations of the world seek these things; and your Father knows that you need them. Instead, seek his Kingdom, and these things shall be yours as well" Lk 12 vs 22 – 31

Oh, how sweet these beautiful living words of a loving God sounds, a loving tender caring Father who means exactly what He says. If only the human race would realize Jesus means exactly what He says because He is God and He is, all problems would have ceased. Having been endowed with God's Grace to realize that God is the Father of humanity who dotes on them and this God is my Father, as I am human, so He dotes on me, therefore, why should I bother when He is there for me and is more than willing to care and provide for me, I said to myself. All I need do is to acknowledge Him and aspire to be what He created me to be, His darling daughter I decided. It is amazing, the more I aspire to be God's loving daughter, which is my true identity, the child of the Almighty God, the identity of humanity, whether the world believes it or not, this beautiful truth remains, the happier and peaceful I became. All the irrelevant things which used to bother me became meaningless and nothing. Before I knew it God transformed me into Love. My whole being became sweet with the longing to bring Jesus to others, that they trust in Him, love Him and allow Him to transform them also. Daily reading of the Bible gradually became a habit and the more I read the more it comes alive to me, drawing me closer to our Heavenly Father, to the God who created me.

Somehow I felt within me the urge to know more about Saints whose lives fascinated me thereby, consequently generating strongly in me the desire to become a Saint, a close friend of Jesus in whose love I intend, at all cost, to abide, by His grace now and forever. I said to myself the Saints are also human beings like myself, my brothers and sisters who realized the depth of the Eternal Father's Love, gave up everything to assist Jesus fight for the Father's Kingdom, so what stops me from joining the chorus, hence the Father loves me that much as well. Having become aware of this I can hardly think of nothing else but Jesus. I fell head over heels in love with Him realizing all He forfeited and suffered for love of me. I became His prisoner of Love. The desire for Sainthood itself, surged in me the beauty of life in the supernatural, the Divine Life, awakening my consciousness to the reality my place is not of this world rather there where the Eternal Father is, with Jesus, in Jesus and for Jesus. Everything began to make sense as I realized I am alive in Jesus. Life becomes suddenly beautiful living for Jesus, having crucified self on His Holy Cross and offered it to Him. To my utter surprise death suddenly becomes sweet, something to look forward to and I understood my brother Saint Francis of Assisi calling death "sister death" Yes, indeed she is sister death, a welcomed August sister to be loved for her sweet kindness in being the venue through which we ascend to our Eternal Father. She is no longer dreadful but a welcomed sister, to come whenever it pleases the Father to call me Home to His Heavenly Kingdom, into Eternal Joy, to rest eternally on His Most Wonderful, Most Beautiful, Most Loving fatherly Bosom, throughout Eternity. Oh, what an Eternal Heavenly Bliss to look forward to.

The death of my father was a turning point in my life. It was then I realized the vacuum in my poor life. For someone who was doted on by her parents I was living a dog's life, a life I would say was partially the handwriting of fate and partially my own making. It was the handwriting of fate as I became a prey to the effect of the Nigerian civil war which threw me into the trap of a Catholic priest who used his charm to seduce a teenage girl simply due to relief material to which he had access from the caritas. The allusion of this stain on my person, as being partially my fault, is due to my incapability of continual resistance to the seductive attempts of the seducer, which was expected of me, as he was a priest of God. Thus Satan saw it as a weapon against my father, a devout and righteous Christian, though not Catholic then, but our most merciful Father made him one just before He called him home, who led a simple and humble life in the fear of God, a civil servant, with substantial income to give his family a comfortable existence, who would have used his position to enrich himself, being in control of government money in his locality, but he would not dare, rather he chose to assist the poor as much as he could, procuring them with jobs and otherwise. The enemy of God and humanity, Satan, through his subordinates led me into the tutelage of his agent from which our loving and merciful Father rescued me, nullified a marriage that never existed, as light and darkness have nothing in common, baptized me with living water directly from Heaven, put back the clock and embraced me in a very special way. This horrible experience is narrated in details in my book "Loving God". Every priest should take his vocation more seriously, keeping his focus on Jesus, his Divine Master, and put flesh under subjection, like St. Paul did, renew regularly his priestly vows, spend time before the Blessed Sacrament, and rely on our Blessed Mother for assistance.

Priestly vocation in itself is a beautiful mystery which no priest should take for granted. Should one lose Eternal salvation for a moment of pleasure, for lust? Why should someone who knows the truth say to himself "let me commit sin after I will go for confession" forgetting God does not deceive nor can He be deceived. No one is exempted from hell. The Almighty Father is truly abundant in Mercy, and also a just judge. As St. Paul rightly puts it, we should not remain in sin that grace may abound. God is too good a Father, He does not deserve the treatment He is given. Besides, priests with depraved minds should not stain the image of priesthood. Priesthood is a privilege, to be received with gratitude, serving God in humility with respect and awe.

One would never be able to realize how sweet and wonderful our Heavenly Father is until one surrenders completely to Him in Jesus with complete trust. I was fortunate to be raised by very humble parents, although not Catholics, but they practiced the Catholic virtue of humility, mercy and uniting suffering with the sufferings of Jesus. They instilled in me the fear of God which sustained me as I was tossed through many waters. Having had a good parental upbringing, the love for my parents earned me a deep strong love for God. It is indeed amazing that at my age I am a child, the Heavenly Father's child. Having been won by God with His fatherly love I realized what a wonderful Father He is accepting me with such warm embrace as though I am such a special child, although I am such an unworthy, wretched, nothing, a nobody, less than half of an ant, a Cinderella. The Almighty God accepted me with Arms wide open, into His warm embrace, in my sinfulness, like "the prodigal son".

I am indeed overwhelmed with our Heavenly Father's love. My life as a whole has turned into thanksgiving to God for being such a wonderful Father. I thank Him for being who He is, for being God, for all His Virtues that comprise His Beauty which I adore from the very depth of my heart.

However, somehow, I got over the shock of my father's departure, as a sense of peace enveloped me with the assurance my father was not dead when I remembered "God is not God of the dead but of the living". This conviction won me the assurance my father is in Heaven. God in His infinite Mercy confirmed it to me in a beautiful dream in which Jesus and my father appeared together, in the sky, low enough for me to behold them clearly. My father then descended to take a seat in the balcony of my apartment. In due time, I realized Jesus sent my father, as an Angel, to assist me in the difficulties I was facing under the Satan's agent. As I mentioned above the details can be read in my book "loving God" For my peace of mind, Jesus appeared together with my father for me to know my father is with Him in Heaven and that He sent Him to me.

In the course of time I began to realize my love for my father is actually meant for God. In the healthy father daughter relationship I had with my father I was to learn from it how to love God who is my Father and the Father of my father. Parents, therefore, are obliged to show love to the children entrusted into their care by the Almighty Father to enable them learn to love Him who created them. However, before I knew it, I was forging a relationship with God the Father in Jesus Christ. Gradually God the Father began to replace the position of my biological father without affecting my love for him, who though no longer in sight but present in spirit as He is with God the Father in Jesus Christ in Heaven. Thereafter, my life began to blossom in union with the Holy Trinity through Jesus Christ who dwells in me. To the Joy of my heart my life became fulfilled, as I began living with the Living God just like everyone living with his parents. Indeed there is nothing impossible with God, all there is to it is Trust, complete surrender to God of Creation to whom humanity owes her existence. One is endowed with as much as one offers as love is a selfless giving of oneself in sacrifice and in humility. It hurts, at the same time sweet, in painless perfection at her ultimate destination in the Glory of God.

When I saw, on EWTN, the joy on the face of a musician who was rejoicing his mother gave him a chance to live, despite her raping experience, in his pro-life advert, in which he displayed a family photograph with the inscription "My children adore me" I was impressed by the thrill he showed over his family life. Thereafter, I felt deep sorrow, overwhelmed with pity for the Almighty God Who loves us with a motherly love, Who would stop at nothing for the happiness of His Beloved Children, yearning for the surrender of their hearts to Him who created them. How sadly do we forget He would also want to say, in ecstasy, just like that musician "My Children adore me." However, kneeling down in prayer, pondering over that advert, tears rolled down my cheeks. It was God's Tears! Little do we realize the pain we cause God. How sad, a great number of God's Children deny Him their heart, oblivious of the depth of the agony of the Most Sacred Heart of Jesus due to their estrangement. If the adoration of our children, who are not actually our children but God's, is a source of such joy to our hearts why do we deny God who is the Father of us all the same joy over us His rightful children. God has feelings. The little things parents appreciate from their children would not be less appreciated by God from us, as we are His children. On the long run, such little things would help us avoid sin due to the continual thoughts on how to please God the Father who would always lend a helping Hand through the Sacraments Jesus lovingly provided, as a loving Father, to assist us, His Children on our pilgrim journey to our Eternal Home in Him, with him and for Him. This way the enemy and his subordinates would be put to shame and confounded. In so doing we help hasten Christ's glorious reign of peace.

That the Almighty God, Lord of Heaven and Earth, Creator of all that is, seen and unseen created me and gave His Heart to me is indeed overwhelming. Honestly, contemplating God`s Goodness and fatherly Love, considering the nonchalant attitude most of His children give Him, tears run down my cheeks. Amazingly, the Beloved Heavenly Dad does not even allow me to weep. He turns my tears into His, which I regard as His kisses and I kiss them. Our Heavenly Dad is indeed a Dad to be proud of. I am very proud of Him and so must you. He is the best Dad. I deem myself most fortunate to be the child of God. Oh, What a marvelous feeling of security and Hope to be the child of the Most High God.

God the Father is within reach as He is Omnipresent. He resides in us, in me, in my heart. He is in Jesus Christ whom I receive in the Eucharist. After it dawned on me God has feelings, having created me in His image, therefore, as my Father and the Father of all, He expects everyone to care for Him the way we care for our biological fathers who in the real sense are not our fathers, but our brothers, our guardians, hence God is the Father of all fathers and our Father. This realization made me aware my biological father's role was to take care of me for God my Father, the way St. Joseph took care of the Holy Child Jesus for the Almighty Father, therefore, I should love God more than I loved my biological father. If I loved God more than my biological father and cared about His feelings, then I must think twice before doing anything, making sure it would not displease the Father whom I love above everything, above anybody and above myself. This awareness paved way for a real Father, daughter relationship with God the Father and won me complete confidence in Him. I began to live with God the Father in the Belief He will surely take care of me His little girl, His darling daughter, His little Mary of the Most Sacred Heart of Jesus, His child. I live with my Heavenly Parents, with Jesus and Mary as though they are physically present and the Holy Angels watch over us. Therefore, I never take a step without informing Jesus, Mum and Dad. It works because My Father in Heaven has taught me to trust Him like a baby in its mother's arms. Should anything happen to me, then it is my Father's Holy Will and His Holy Will is Love. Now I am alive because I live, I live in Jesus, in Love, I'm in love with love. Oh, what a beautiful feeling to allow oneself be transformed into love. One begins indeed here below to feel Heaven. God Himself takes care of everything and burden becomes light, relief obtained, peace achieved, Hope born, and Death becomes a welcomed august visitor, a friend, the bearer of sweet expectations in Heavenly Bliss. This is profound tranquility that only the Beloved Heavenly Father can grant in Jesus Christ.

On the cross Jesus gave us a final beautiful gift, His Mother, the blessed Virgin Mary. In this way He made us His brothers and sisters. Thus revealing the venue by which His Most Sacred Heart could be easily reached. Definitely Jesus is the way to the Father, but Jesus has to be reached in order to reach the Father and the shortest way to reach Jesus is through His Mother. Realizing this, thanks to the Grace of God, the blessed Virgin became my Mother, and my Girl-friend. I do not only see Her as the Mother of Jesus, but my Mother too and when I say my Mother, I mean my biological Mother. You Know, this might sound funny and silly but Jesus said if you have faith like a mustard seed it will move mountain, therefore, I asked for the Grace to love Her the way Jesus loves Her and it was granted me, although no-one can actually love Her the way Jesus loves Her, but almost the way He loves Her. I love the Blessed Virgin more than I love my biological mother hence she is the Mother of us all. She is the most loving Mother one can ever think of and I love Her as the little sister of Jesus. I am Her little girl, Her little Mary of the Most Sacred Heart of Jesus, Her child. There is nothing impossible with God. Oh, how fortunate I am living with my Most Loving Heavenly Parents, with Dad, Mum, elder Brother and Bridegroom, though in Heaven they be, yet here below with me, their child, their little Mary of the Most Sacred Heart of Jesus. I have nothing to fear because I have my Parents protective watchful eyes, the protective watchful eyes of my elder Brother and Bridegroom. What can be so safe to a girl as to have her Mother as her Girl-friend. The Blessed Virgin Mary is Mother and Girl-friend to me.

> Oh Mum, sweet beautiful Mum, Queen of my heart,
> most sweetest, tender, loving Mum that ever is and
> ever will be. How is it, the most sweetest loving Mum

of God my Mum be. Oh, priceless fortune, my sweet delight, such tenderness, your smile be to this poor unworthy little nothing me, less than half of an ant.

May you, dearest Mum, suckle me, your child, your little Mary of the Most Sacred Heart of Jesus, as you suckled your Beloved Son, Jesus, my elder Brother, so would your Virtues be infused in me O Blessed Virgin, my Mum, then Jesus, Bridegroom Most Charming, Most Beloved, Divine Son Thine, Beloved mine, Savior so sweet, in me His Bride, Your Reflections beholds, for sweet moments of Bliss with His Bride. O sweet passionate moments of love with the Divine.

Thus shall He, O Immaculate Queen of my heart, Mum most dear, His Reflection, in me, His sweet Bride, with His beautiful dreamy eyes delightfully beholds, that joy, O joy of sweet delight, His Most Sacred Heart envelopes, in union with poor, little, wretched, nothing unworthy me, less than half of an ant, His Cinderella, His Bride, with sweet sensations thrills, in the ocean of the sweet flavor of His Love, in perfect ecstasy.

It might all sound funny, but there is actually nothing funny about it, because Truth is Reality and Jesus is the Way the Truth and the Life. Jesus tenderly taught me to trust Him like a baby in its mother's arms. Thereafter, I surrendered completely to His Divine Will, thanks to His Divine Mercy. He is the Love of my life, Most Beloved of my heart, my Hero, my Divine Master, my darling sweet All and All. We share everything together, joys and sorrows, no exception. We suffer together and enjoy together. Jesus said "abide in my love" to abide in His love is to keep His commandments, doing so, one experiences His love. When it dawned on me, due to God's Mercy, Jesus compared the Kingdom of Heaven with little children, although, on the other hand St. Paul in 1 Corinth.13 wrote "when I became a man I gave up childish things" I realized I am a grown up, but for the Kingdom of God I must be a child. If God is my Father, then I am His child. A child is always a child to his parents it does not matter how old he or she is. The true meaning of these words of Jesus "the Kingdom of God is like little children" was granted me. This saying of Jesus has a deeper meaning I thought. Just be the child that you are, love being God's child, His little girl, His darling daughter, His little Mary of the Most Sacred Heart of Jesus, His Princess, Dad's darling. It is well known children do not bear grudges, they easily forgive and forget the wrong done to them, of course, that is Christian principle, but there is more to it. To achieve this "more" requires God's Grace, prayer and total submission of self to God, uniting ones will to God's Holy Will in humble trust. Then the scripture becomes alive, the words of Jesus are alive, they are living water, they are words of God, they are Jesus. Heaven begins here on earth, Jesus is Heaven, union with Him here on earth is Heaven. Be not afraid, simply trust, persevere, hope, pray, be merciful, forgiving, patient, embrace the cross and keep focus on Jesus.

"You are of more value than sparrows" are not mere words. They are the key to my relationship with Jesus. They are Reality and Truth. They simply mean what they depict. What Jesus says is. Sometimes one tends to forge a relationship with Jesus and forgets the Father who is the Father of Jesus and our Father too. Jesus once said "be not afraid, it is the Father's Will to give you the Kingdom" thereby revealing to us the Father's Will, Heaven belongs to us. What a wonderful, compassionate, loving Father God is. If God sacrificed His only begotten Son for love of me, I thought, there is nothing He would not do for me, I realized. Nevertheless, I realized also the necessity to meet God half way for He is the Father of us all, but I needed to see Him as my Father, I needed a personal relationship with Him. The Holy Trinity is a dogma of the Church as was revealed by Jesus Christ Himself. In the Holy Trinity there is only one God but three Persons therefore, God the Father and God the Holy Spirit are in Jesus. They dwell in the Most Sacred Heart of Jesus. I then said to myself, if I have a personal relationship with Jesus what stops me from having a personal relationship with God the Father. The need for a personal relationship with the Father, I realized, is portrayed in Mary Magdalene's encounter with Jesus after His resurrection. After Jesus revealed Himself to her at the tomb, in the attempt to hold Him Jesus said to her "Do not hold me, for I have not yet ascended to the Father, but go to my brethren and say to them, I am ascending to my Father and to your Father, to my God and to your God" What a blessing to humanity! This golden revelation of having equal right with Jesus to the fathership of God is a priceless treasure that Jesus bestowed on humanity which should not be disregarded. Jesus is our Friend, our Brother, our Everything and God remains our Father. A most wonderful, loving, patient, trustworthy, faithful, compassionate, good God and above all infinitely Merciful.

God dotes on His children, there is nothing He will not do for them. He would go to any length for their happiness and you know what, I am extremely proud of my Dad and very fascinated in Him like a little child as I love and cherish Him with the heart and mind of a child. I admire God my Father. He is a wonderful Father. His love for me overwhelms me. His love for me arouses a defensive instinct in me, such as is seen in little children when anyone attacks or insults their father. This causes sadness in my poor little heart which refuses to understand the treatment He is given, as though He has no feelings, although He has the most tender of Heart, worrying about the well-being of His children who are blinded and carried away with the pomp and riches of this world, dancing to the tune of the enemy whose ultimate abode is hell. One should not forget we do not belong to this world as we are all on pilgrimage towards our final destination which is Heaven. If God's love for us made Him sacrifice His only son for our salvation, why not trust in His Love and inherit the Kingdom He has prepared for you? If God could do so much for you with the sacrifice of His only begotten Son as proof of His Love for you why not bear a little suffering as proof of your love for Him, your Father? Don't you realize Satan in his frustration, aware of his defeat, is only playing a game of deceit on you to land you in perdition to spend eternity with him in hell, so that you lose Eternal life in Heaven with your Eternal Father, is that what you want?

In His third appearance to His Disciples, Jesus called them His children, although they were all His elder except John, the youngest and beloved Apostle. It was the Father in Him who spoke, "Children, have you any fish?" He asked them, so having none, He bade them "Cast the net on the right side of the boat, and you will find some." With their obedience they were blessed with so many fishes, surprised the net did not break. In order to please God and abide in His Love obedience is essential in humble trust. In total surrender to God's love one discovers His commandments are not difficult. A heart in love bears all things, seeks for the good and comfort of the beloved. God is a Father who derives pleasure in serving the children He created for himself and for love. Could you imagine the Almighty Father, I AM, the Supreme Being, the Supreme Majesty preparing breakfast for His Apostles? That is exactly what He did when Jesus asked them to bring some of the fish they caught and come and have breakfast. Fancy how it would be in Heaven, in His heavenly abode, where He is waiting patiently and eagerly to embrace His faithful children who accept Him by returning love for Love. What He has in store for man eyes have not seen nor have ears heard. There is therefore, the need for perseverance in order to assist the Lord Jesus pull us to Heaven. Without the trust in His Love and in His Divine Mercy it spells failure. "Resist the devil and he will flee from you" It would be too sad to miss the Father's Home where He is waiting patiently with Love.

God's tender loving nature is not meant for Heaven only but to be also experienced in this terrifying wilderness to reach its perfection in Heaven. Why then offend such a loving Father. "I have delight in the human race" the Lord said. His attachment and love for the human race will never cease. It is only proper to be on the side of the Lord against

His enemy, against Satan, also man's enemy. The enemy of one's Father is one's enemy as well, therefore, stop SIN. Our Heavenly Father hates sin so Satan dares entangle us with sin to lure us to his way to the displeasure of God, our Beloved Heavenly Father. As children who love their father aim at pleasing their father, so it is simply natural to consider God's feelings, as His loving and subordinate children should, keep His commandments, for our own benefit, please Him and help wipe away the tears in His eyes. Is it not high time humanity became wise, stop the enemy from deceiving them, from making them, who are God's children, help him hurt their Beloved Father? Why not turn the back at the enemy whose wicked intension is to stop the Almighty God, our Father, from enjoying us as His children? Why can't we realize God created us for Himself? For His pleasure, for Love? As transient is the smile of the pomp and riches of this world why run after them and fail to make provision in Heaven for the soul in Joy Eternal, in Jesus Christ, the Way, the Truth and the Life?

CHAPTER IV

THE BODY OF CHRIST

"I have said this to you, that in me you may have peace. In the world you have tribulation; but be of good cheer, I have overcome the world" Jesus lifted up his eyes to heaven and made the following wonderful prayer expressing the deepest desire of His Most Sacred Heart for the unity of Christendom. The aim of every Christian therefore, must be to swallow pride and aspire for the realization of the desire of the Beloved Savior, as such a gesture portrays in itself a genuine act of love for the Beloved. To act otherwise is nothing but fake and selfish love which the Divine Beloved does not deserve and does not cherish. For an honest and true discipleship, pleasing to Jesus Christ, one must possess the noble virtues of humility, and obedience without which we labor in vain deceiving ourselves. God cannot be deceived nor does He deceive. He despises lip service. To love Jesus is to observe His precepts, put Him first above everything, above everyone and above self.

"Father, the hour has come; glorify thy Son that the Son may glorify thee, since thou hast given him power over all flesh, to give eternal life to all whom thou hast given him. And this is eternal life, that they know thee the only true God and Jesus Christ whom thou hast sent. I glorified thee on earth, having accomplished the work which thou gavest me to do; and now, Father, glorify thou me in thy own presence with the glory which I had with thee before the world was made.

"I have manifested thy name to the men whom thou gavest me out of the world; thine they were, and thou gavest them to me, and they have kept thy word. Now they know that everything that thou hast given me is from thee; for I have given them the words which thou gavest me, and they have received them and know in truth that I came from thee; and they have believed that thou didst send me. I am praying for them; I am not praying for the world but for those whom thou hast given me, for they are thine; all mine are thine, and thine are mine, and I am glorified in them. And now I am no more in the world, but they are in the world, and I am coming to thee. Holy Father, keep them in thy name, which thou hast given me, that they might be one, even as we are one. While I was with them, I kept them in thy name, which thou hast given me, and none of them is lost but the son of perdition, that the scripture might be fulfilled. But now I am coming to thee; and these things I speak in the world, that they may have my joy fulfilled in themselves. I have given them thy word; and the world has hated them because they are not of the world, even as I am not of the world. I do not pray that thou shouldst take them out of the world, but that thou shouldst keep them from the evil one. They are not of the world, even as I am not of the world. Sanctify them in the truth; thy word is truth. As thou didst send me into the world, so I have sent them into the world. And for their sake I consecrate myself, that they also may be consecrated in the truth.

"I do not pray for these only, but also for those who believe in me through their word, that they may all be one; even as thou, Father, art in me, and I in thee, that they also may be in us, so that the world may believe that thou hast sent me. The glory which thou hast given me I have given to them, that they may be one even as we are one, I in them and thou in me, that they may become perfectly one so that the world may know that thou hast sent me and hast loved them even as thou hast loved me. Father, I desire that they also, whom thou hast given me, may be with me where I am, to behold my glory which thou hast given me in thy love for me before the foundation of the world. O righteous Father, the world has not known thee; but I have known thee; and these know that thou hast sent me. I made known to them thy name, and I will make it known, that the love with which thou hast loved me may be in them and I in them" Jn 17 vs 1 – end.

In Christendom, there is an urgent need to ponder on the motivation of our Lord Jesus Christ in making such a heart-rending prayer. This prayer is neither a display of emotion nor are they mere words but rather the conveyance of His Divine intention for humanity. It portrays the Divine desire of our Lord for the unity of His mystical Body, the Church. He wants an intimate relationship with Her members, they should know and love the Eternal Father who dwells in Him. Being one with the Eternal Father in whom He in turn dwells, as one God, the Almighty God desires one Church. It is an agonizing predicament for the Most Sacred Heart of Jesus seeing His Body, the Church turn into pieces. The Almighty God is a God of unity. He is one God yet a triune God. Everything He does ends up in one unit, one body. Take for instance marriage "For this reason shall a man leave his father's house and be joined to his wife and both of them shall be one" just as He is one though three. "I am the vine and you are the branches" The Christian fold are members of His mystical body. Nobody wants his body to be torn in pieces, neither does Jesus. Christianity is not what we make of it but what Jesus wants it to be. Of course, the scripture says "Believe in the Lord Jesus Christ and you will be saved" unfortunately it does not stop there. To believe in the Lord Jesus Christ means to believe in all that He stands for therefore, keeping His commandments in order to abide in His Love. An important commandment of His is to be one as He is one with the Father. Christendom should be one unit, united like the God-head, God the Father, God the Son and God the Holy Spirit, three persons, one God. In Christendom the Church is the mother, Christians are the children and Jesus is the Head of the Church. There is Mother, children, God, all one in Jesus Christ, hence the Church is His mystical Body. Jesus prayed for the Church to be one in Him and being one in Him we are automatically one in the Holy Trinity. What a wonderful beautiful inheritance, to share with God in His Divinity, unworthy though we all are. A marvelous gift of God which no one should come short of. A priceless treasure worth every sacrifice to possess, a life with God, in God and for God eternally in Eternity. What a heavenly Bliss that would be – Don't miss it! It didn't matter how sinful members of His mystical Body are, He came for sinners, the Sacraments He left are there in His Church for sanctifying grace. As we are all sinners we are not fit to point accusing fingers at the Church, doing so would be pointing fingers at our Lord who is the Church. To separate the weeds from the wheat is the work of Angels when the harvest is ripe. All it takes is to remain in the Vine and belong to the Vine therefore, cut away branches should have themselves engrafted in the Vine to belong to the Vine, to belong to the Family of God, the new Israel of the new Covenant, the CHURCH, not churches.

If we believe Jesus is truly God and truly Man then we must believe His words never returns back to Him empty. Therefore, it is baffling some Christians fail to accept the Church He founded still exists, the Church to whom He promised to be with until the end of the world. If they did they would have remained realizing God does not make empty promises because He is God. "They went out from us because they are not of us, if they were they would have remained with us" When God says, it is! Jesus founded a Church which the gate of hell cannot prevail against. He never said the gate of hell will not try, which it has been doing all the centuries, but it will not prevail. Trusting in the Holy Word of God is strength and life. One cannot put a deaf ear to God's promise because the enemy took an advantage of the sinful nature of the members of His Mystical Body, the Church, and planted weeds in Her midst to desert the Church for whom He shed His Precious Blood to found. To start another church is disobedience to the Eternal Word, to the Almighty God, making oneself liable to building on the foundation of another. Let's not forget Jesus is truly God and truly man, some sects, like the Jehovah's witnesses who take Him to be an "Archangel," would not agree. However, the testimony Jesus bore of Himself should not be ignored.

"whoever has seen me has seen the Father," everyone should realize that when Jesus says, it is. His words will never return empty to Him. He is God, the Alpha and the Omega, the Almighty.

Consequent to the irrelevant answers of His Apostles to His question "Who do men say that I am" Jesus asked "But who do you say that I am?" Simon Peter replied "You are the Christ, the Son of the living God" to which Jesus responded "Blessed are you, Simon Bar-Jona! For flesh and blood has not revealed this to you, but my Father who is in heaven. And I tell you, you are Peter, and on this rock I will build my church, and the powers of death shall not prevail against it. I will give you the keys of the kingdom of heaven, and whatever you bound on earth shall be bound in heaven, and whatever you loose on earth shall be loosed in heaven" These are God's Words, God speaks. Jesus means every word He spoke. A straight forward statement, not in parable, spoken clearly for everyone to understand. He knew He would go back to the Father in Heaven and needed a visible head for His Church. Just as He said He did not come to change the law but to fulfill it so, as a Jew, being in the line of David He acted as such. As the kings in the line of David gave the keys of the kingdom to an Overseer in their absence, the same way Jesus gave the keys of the kingdom of Heaven to Peter as the visible head of His Church, His Kingdom on earth, which is the pilgrim Church, part of His Kingdom in Heaven. To found Her He shed His Most Precious Blood and taught us to say the "Our Lord's Prayer," "...Thy Will be done on Earth as it is in Heaven" In Heaven is only One God, three Persons, the Holy Trinity. If the Father's Will should be done on Earth as it is in Heaven, Jesus meant His Church should be one to "give us our daily bread, Jesus Christ in the Eucharist. "He who hears you, hears me" Lk 10:16

Following the removal of the self-seeking Overseer – one over the household – Eliakim, the son of Hilkiah was chosen as the new overseer "In that day I will call my servant Eliakim the son of Hilkiah, and I will clothe him with your robe and will bind your girdle on him and will commit your authority to his hand; and he shall be a father to the inhabitants of Jerusalem and to the house of Judah. And I will place on his shoulder the key of the house of David; he shall open, and none shall shut; and he shall shut, and none shall open. And I will fasten him like a peg in a sure place, and he will become a throne of honor to his father's house" Isaiah 22 vs 20 – 23. The seat of Peter, the bearer of the keys, in the Vatican foretold.

The papal seat is a throne of honor, a privilege to suffer for the love of Jesus, shouldering His burden, strengthening and tending the sheep as Jesus commanded Him when He asked Peter three times if he loved Him. The Pope is the servant of the Children of God just as Jesus came to serve. He is the Vicar of Christ, the Overseer of God's Kingdom on earth, a symbol of unity, Peter being the first Pope. If the Church which Jesus founded failed to have a continuous existence and is unable to withstand the trials of time, then Jesus is not true, but if she does, then He is truly God whose words never return to Him empty. The fact is, the Church which Jesus founded on Peter still exists, gate of hell will never prevail against Her. Jesus founded only one Church not churches, in order to find out which Church that Church is, simply look out for the Pope. Where the Pope is there the Church Jesus founded is. As there is only one true God, there is also only one true Church, the Roman Catholic Church.

Christianity is not a commodity to be commercialized. An honest believer in Jesus Christ, who loves Him, and desires the attainment of eternal salvation would genuinely seek to serve Him in obedience to His Holy Will, which is to keep His commandments in order to abide in His Love. "If you keep my commandments, you will abide in my love, just as I have kept my Father's commandments and abide in his love" There are two ultimate goals for humanity, eternal salvation in Heaven with Jesus, in Jesus and for Jesus or eternal death in hell with Satan and for Satan. Therefore, there is urgent need to give the choice we make a thorough thought, as the future state of the soul is decided here on this exile, on earth, by our individual free-will. If we find it natural to please someone we love because we desire to always be loved by him, in some cases, we even tolerate from him, what we would otherwise not have tolerated if we did not love him, trying to please him as he desires to be pleased in order to remain loved by him, why then is it difficult to realize Jesus is not different. He created us in His own image for Himself, therefore it would be wise to please Him the way He wants to be pleased and not the way we want to please Him. Jesus desires the unity of His Mystical Body. To break away from His Mystical Body is going against His Holy Will in the first place. His Most Sacred Heart is grieved seeing how His Mystical Body is torn into pieces. To abandon Him, the Church, to found another, it did not matter how the ears of your followers are tickled with fables, with promises of material wealth, and good health, it is an offence to our Lord. It leaves His Most Sacred Heart in agony. "When a blind man leads the blind both of them fall into the pit." Jesus loves you, He created you for love therefore, return to your roots with your followers, to the One, Holy, Catholic, and Apostolic Church He founded if indeed you love Him and are zealous for Him. Otherwise, "What will it profit a man to gain the whole world and loose his soul" Heaven is worth fighting for and Jesus desires everyone to make Heaven, give him the chance to lead you Home to Him in Heaven, to the Eternal Father. The decision is yours. It would be a pity if you missed Heaven on your own choice. A word is enough for the wise. Do not allow soap into your eyes while you are in water.

Jesus Christ, Himself God, did not come into the world as a rich man, but as a pauper in order to set an example riches of this world are transitory, and not to be pursued. Suffering is a part of Christian life, after all Jesus emptied Himself out for us on His Holy Cross. His Suffering, the extent of the pain He bore on His blessed body, physically and mentally would never be fully known, but one must realize it was an unimaginable and unbearable pain which He would not have been able to bear, in

His Humanity, had it not been for His Most Sacred Heart, the burning Furnace of Love, the seat of Divine Mercy, from where He drew his unbreakable Will, courage and strength, coupled with His determination to fulfil the Father's Will. With this on mind every Christian is expected to take up his cross and follow Him. There is no need to seek the easy way out, to found another church contrary to the one He founded with His Most Precious Blood, and serve Him in a more comfortable way, in your own way. That is wrong! it is not God's way. Jesus did not choose the easy way but rather obedient to the Father even unto death. As His disciple, it is expected also of you, if need be, to empty yourself out for Him for love of Him.

It is naive and thoughtless to assume the notion, Church does not save' because it does. For those whose Christianity is based only on the Bible, do you not realize the falacity in the interpretation of that Bible which has led to thousands of churches? Jesus never said one should make out one's own interpretation and do what one wants with it. Failure to comply to the ordinances set up by Jesus Christ Himself for His Church spells danger. He clearly instructed, no one should make himself a judge as judgement is for God alone. The parable of the Weeds among the Wheat portrays the Church He was to found on Peter whose name He changed to Rock. "The Kingdom of Heaven may be compared to a man who sowed good seed in his field; but while men were sleeping, his enemy came and sowed weeds among the wheat, and went away. So when the plants came up and bore grain, then the weeds appeared also. And the servants of the householder came and said to him, 'Sir, did you not sow good seed in your field, how then has it weeds?' He said to them, 'An enemy has done this.' The servants said to him, 'Then do you want us to go and gather them?' But he said, 'No; lest in gathering the weeds you uproot the wheat along with them. Let both grow together until the harvest; and at harvest time I will tell the reapers, gather the weeds first and bind them in bundles to be burned, but gather the wheat into my barn.'" Matt. 13 vs 24 – 30

So also the parable of the Sower "And when a great crowd came together and people from town after town came to him, he said in a parable: "A sower went out to sow his seed; and as he sowed, some fell along the path, and was trodden under foot, and the birds of the air devoured it. And some fell on the rock; and as it grew up, it withered away, because it had no moisture. And some fell among thorns; and the thorns grew with it and choked it. And some fell into good soil and grew, and yielded a hundred-fold" as he said this he called out, "He who has ears to hear, let him hear" and when his disciples asked him what this parable meant, he said, "To you it has been given to know the secrets of the kingdom of God; but for others they are in parables, so that seeing they may not see, and hearing they may not understand" Lk 8 vs 4 – 10

The word of God is not of private interpretation. The right for the interpretation of the Scripture for spiritual nourishment of the Children of God, for spiritual guidance, has been entrusted to the Church by Jesus Christ Himself whose mystical Body the Church is. In this way His Mystical Body, the Church, whose soul is the Holy Spirit, is meant to remain one, though many members, in order to avoid misinterpretation of the gospel. The oneness of the Church enables all Her members to be nourished and sanctified with the Sacraments. The parable of the sower refers to the seed as the word of God, the ones along the path are those who heard, but then the devil takes away the word from their heart to prevent them from believing for their salvation. The ones that fell on the rock are those who received the word with joy, but have no root, they believed for a while and are unable to withstand temptation. As for those which fell on thorns, they hear the word of God, but have no backbone as they are entangled on their way with the cares, riches and pleasures of life which prevents their fruit from germinating. Finally, those that fell on good soil are those who, hearing the word of God treasure it in an honest and good heart, consequently bringing forth fruit with patience. They are those who remain in the One, Holy, Catholic and Apostolic Church founded by Jesus Christ, bringing forth fruits, realizing God's promise, that gate of hell will not prevail against His Church, and for this reason remained, believing God would surely take care of every heresy, sieve out all incorrect ideologies to stabilize the doctrine of the Church. After all, a child does not begin at once to walk from the cradle, he crawls, stands and with unsteady steps gradually learns to walk as he gains balance.

It is cowardice to abandon our Divine Master, like in the garden of Gethsemane when He needed consolation. Instead of those who say they belong to Him holding unto the Virtue of patience, trusting in Him who is most Trustworthy and most Faithful and persevere, He is once again abandoned. How disappointing! After all, it is for love of us He founded His Church, for our own good, that we may feed on Him in order to get rid of traces of sin and be transformed into Love and be like Him so as to inherit the Kingdom of God prepared for us from the foundation of the world. Furthermore, selfishness, greed, pride, lack of patience and trust in our Lord Jesus Christ gave rise to the existence of so many churches in our world today despite our Lords plea we should be one as He is one with the Father so that the world may know we belong to Him. The existence of so many Churches gave rise to atheism, when men began to deceive themselves, partially due to the confusion caused by the existence of so many churches which made it somewhat difficult to differentiate the good from the bad, being faced with the question "Which one is true," resulting to not accepting any at all and jump into the conclusion "there is no God," also due to the individual incapability of self-knowledge, and due to mere egotism, allowing oneself be blinded by Satan whose objective is to deprive men a share in the Divine Life of God. What he, Satan, cannot have no one should. Jesus desperately desires, for all humanity, Eternal life with Him in Him and for Him in His Heavenly Kingdom with the Eternal Father. There is no excuse for anyone who does not believe in the existence of God for man is created with intellect, with reason, the ability to wonder, in awe, at the wisdom of creation and admire the beauty of nature, consequently realize there must be a Creator, for such beauty. The magnificence of the cosmos could not have been without the touch of the Supernatural, without God. His creation is a proof of His existence. Human being is a proof of the existence of God. It is a sin not to believe in God, otherwise how would one expect to share in the life of One whom he does not believe exists. Humanity is most fortunate to have a most loving and good God, who pardons all the profanations, indifferences, sacrileges and atrocities to His person if only His pardon is penitently sought for. Failure to accept His Divine Mercy now maybe too late. Everyone is a sinner, no one merits God's Mercy but He grants it due to His infinite Love for humanity, due to the ocean of His Divine Mercy and Goodness. However, make hay while the sun shines, accept His Divine Mercy with gratitude, with respect and awe. "Judge not and je shall not be judged" accept the Pope, the Vicar of Jesus Christ, after all, He instituted the Papacy himself. God exists!

"Those who are whole need no physician", "Teacher, this woman has been caught in the act of adultery. Now in the law Moses commanded us to stone such. What do you say of her?" Jesus replied "let him Who is without sin among you be the first to throw stone at her" Jesus came to find what was lost. His mystical Body, the Church as a Mother nourishes Her children, members of His mystical Body with the Sacraments, sanctifying and transforming them as their Eternal Bridegroom, preparing them for the heavenly banquet, the wedding of the Lamb, when He will be perfectly united with His brides. The segregation from the One Holy Catholic and Apostolic Church founded by Jesus to found another church, was a big mistake as it gave rise to sects and thousands of churches to the displeasure of God. It does not comply to His Holy Will, "Let them be one as we are one." This deprives these sects and churches from the Sacraments of sanctifying Grace, the Holy Eucharist and the Sacrament of Reconciliation which is the Mercy Seat of God. The ministers of these churches and sect have no authority to officiate as they deprived themselves the right of apostolic succession. There is only one God, therefore there is only one Church, hence the Church is the Body of Jesus Christ. The Church is like the Ark of Noah in which only those in the Ark were saved. Church saves, the One Holy Catholic and Apostolic Church founded by Jesus, on Peter the Rock, saves, She is the Body of Christ, She is Jesus, Jesus saves. The Church is in the possession of the whole Truth. She has the seven Sacraments instituted by Jesus Christ Himself.

Nevertheless, it does not mean those who remain in mortal sin have automatic salvation, no, but they have asset to the Sacraments, provided by Jesus Christ, which render to the soul sanctifying grace. The Eucharist, if received in a state of grace nourishes the soul. Then from the Sacrament of reconciliation, God's Mercy Seat, sinners receive healing for their sick souls, makes them ready to receive their Lord in the Holy Eucharist. This does not mean one should remain in sin that grace may abound. "Let me sin after I will go for confession" would be deceiving one self. However, those outside the Church, not on their own fault, have the opportunity of salvation also if their Christian life is in accordance to the teachings of Jesus Christ, having the disposition to please Him, the Lord will surely grant them the opportunity for salvation. He is God, what is impossible for man is possible for God, but why take a chance, why not belong now, keep God's precepts and feel secure.

There is no need beating about the bush, Jesus is the Truth, anyone who loves Him must speak the Truth and the Truth will set him free. The life of many souls are at steak and Jesus wants everyone saved, therefore, Salvation is in the Truth. Anyone who does not make Heaven, after Jesus opened its gate with such bitter passion, is responsible for his own failure. Jesus commanded, we should abide in His Love, to do so is to keep His Commandments. The One, Holy, Catholic and Apostolic Church founded by Jesus on Peter, the Rock, to whom He gave the keys of Heaven, provides the soul with the spiritual nourishment, the Body, Blood, Soul and Divinity of Jesus Christ in the Sacrament of the Eucharist, the Sacrament of His Divine Love. An indispensable nourishment for the soul of every Christian on this pilgrim journey to Life Eternal with Jesus, in Jesus and for Jesus, a sure weapon against the principalities and powers hence we are not fighting only with flesh and blood. His Most Precious Blood, the weapon against the powers of darkness, the price of our Redemption should be honored, adored, reverenced and glorified.

The Church is made up of bundles of sinners, these sinners are members of the Mystical Body of Christ, no one has a right to judge Her but to obey and pray for Her as Jesus is aware of the spiritual condition of Her members. For this reason He left Her with the Sacraments of the Eucharist and Reconciliation for the sanctification of Her members. To pay attention to the wicked enemy, Satan who planted the weeds and allow him feed you with the belief the Church is adulterated and sinful is very precipitous. The Church is Holy. The Church is Jesus. She is His Body. "If we say we have no sin the truth is not in us" To abandon His Church to found another makes one a judge, one throws the first stone as though one has no sin, thereby making Jesus, not only a Liar but also incapable of sustaining His Church till the end of the world as He said. Besides, unable to forgive your brothers, members of His Mystical Body, for whatever grudges you might have against the Holy Church of God, made during the crusade, burning of witches, and during the inquisition, how then do you expect to be forgiven? Forgive and you will be forgiven is clearly stated in the "Our Lord's Prayer" taught by Jesus Christ Himself. Did Jesus say one should quit the Church to found another if such things happened? If so, then, when you believe only on what is written in the bible, where in the bible is such authority given to separate from the Church? Where is it written in the Bible one should believe only on what is written in the Bible? Interestingly, the Bible does support Catholic doctrine on tradition "So then, brethren, stand firm and hold to the traditions which you were taught by us, either by word of mouth or by letter" 2 Thessalonians 2 vs 15. "...the Church of the living God', is the 'pillar and bulwark of the truth...." 1 Timothy 3 vs 15. However, the fact is, those who segregate use such reasoning as a lame excuse to do so, either for economic reasons or for a more comfortable means to profess their religion. In so doing choosing the broad way which Jesus strictly warned against, disbelieving in tradition, whereas the same bible in which they believe states clearly the need to believe in tradition. God is God, what He wants, He wants and nothing and nobody can change that once He wills it, except of course His Divine Mercy. But that is in a different concept. It is the place of man to walk in the precepts of God, not to change them. "As I have warned you when I was going to Macedonia, remain at Ephesus that you may charge certain persons not to teach any different doctrine, nor to occupy themselves with myths and endless genealogies which promote speculations rather than the divine training that is in faith: whereas the aim of our charge is love that issues from a pure heart and a good conscience and sincere faith" 1 Timothy 1 vs 3.

What is Tradition if not what is handed down to the Church orally by the Apostles and by letter as is mentioned above. Our Lord Jesus Christ used the early Church fathers and His Saints to stabilize His Church and put an end to heresy. "Therefore, if we say we have fellowship with Him while we walk in darkness, we lie and do not live according to the truth" 1Jn 1 vs 6. Jesus is tenderly waiting patiently for the reunion of His Mystical Body, for all the strayed sheep, those outside the Catholic Church, to come back to the One, Holy, Catholic and Apostolic Church He established. Give Jesus your heart, allow Him get you acquainted to the Catholic faith. You would be surprised at the richness and the magisterium of the Catholic Church. if it was not necessary for His Church to be one He would not have prayed "...that they may be one as we are one..." God is a triune God, God the Father, God the Son, God the Holy Spirit – The indivisible Trinity, three Persons – One God, therefore, One Church, one Faith and one Baptism. One cannot profess to be a follower of Jesus Christ and keep a deaf ear to His Holy Will. He designed His

Church the way She should function so, She has to function that way, not how individuals or a group of people want Her to function. Jesus is the One Christians follow and serve, every Christian should serve Him then as He desires to be served in order to please Him. Every Christian aims at making Heaven to spend Eternity with Him, this being the case, should not all Christians aspire to keep His precepts to please Him and make Heaven? Should they not reunite? "It is the Father's Will to give you the kingdom" therefore, Jesus wants everyone in Heaven. Don't miss it!

Our good Lord warned that the way to Heaven is narrow, the way to hell broad, many follow it because it is easy, so they avoid the narrow way which appears difficult, but for those who love God it is easy. It is most unfortunate Jesus is in agony, caused by the wounds humanity inflict on Him Who is infinitely in love with them. It causes Him great sorrow seeing so many souls heading for perdition. We must not forget Jesus cannot be less than He is. He is God, God of Love and God of Justice, therefore He must exercise justice. He is a righteous Judge. How wise it is, when the opportunity still exists, while Jesus is still pleading with humanity like a Beggar, to genuinely repent of one's sins, reciprocate His Love, and accept His Divine Mercy. There is need to make hay while the sun shines. He is always ready to stretch out His Hand to assist anyone who reaches out to Him in love. He is eagerly waiting for the slightest attempt made to reach Him in order to pull one to Himself. Heaven is worth any suffering experienced on earth, simply unite it with His suffering. Heaven is a priceless Treasure of Beauty, Love and Tranquility. To be united with God and see Him face to face, live with Him, in Him and for Him as His Beloved Children, what an unfathomable Mercy of God on humanity!

This should arouse a sincere aspiration from the depth of the heart of all humanity for Heaven, thereby expressing the will to appreciate God's Divine Mercy eternally in eternity. It would, perhaps, be advisable to contemplate Life with Jesus in Heaven eternally in Eternity. Life with the Eternal Joy, Lord of Creation, the Highest God, from whom all good things come. What a wonderful life that would be! What an overwhelming Eternal joy! A Life in Love with Love! A Life in Beauty with Beauty! My friend, do not miss it!! Do not allow the pomp and riches of this world, nor lust blind you. Seek to do God's Holy Will. Begin by going back to His Body the Church which He established with the shading of His most Precious Blood. The Church bought with such bitter price! for love of you. There is no need founding another Church, Jesus did not ask for it. Have pity on your Heavenly Father who loves you so much as to sacrifice His only Begotten Son for love of you. Help wipe away the tears from His wonderful fatherly Eyes. Do not allow Him lose you to Satan, His enemy. Remember, He Who is, Who was, and ever will be, cannot be less than He is. He does not deserve it. You are His Heaven. He loves you infinitely. Our God is a Most Merciful God, God of Love. He created you for Love, for Himself. He owns you, yet He calls you "MY CHILD" not "MY SLAVE" Love Him!! Be not afraid! Simply be His Child that you are.

"I am the bread of life. Your fathers ate the manna in the wilderness and they died. This is the bread which comes down from heaven, that a man may eat of it and not die. I am the living bread which came down from heaven; if anyone eats of this bread, he will live forever; and the bread which I shall give for the life of the world is my flesh." The Jews disputed among themselves saying "How can this man give us His flesh to eat?"

Jesus continued and said, "truly, I say to you, unless you eat the flesh of the son of man and drink his blood, you have no life in you; he who eats my flesh and drinks my blood has eternal life, and I will raise him up at the last day for my flesh is food indeed, and my blood is drink indeed. He who eats my flesh and drinks my blood abides in me, and I in him. As the living Father sent me and I live because of the Father, so he who eats me will live because of me. This is the bread which came down from heaven, not such as the fathers ate and died; he who eats this bread will live forever" Jn 6 vs.53 – 58.

The above citation shows clearly the only way to attain Eternal Life is to eat the Flesh of Jesus and drink His blood. The popular slogan of the protestant and sectarian churches "Believe in the Lord Jesus Christ and be saved" does not end there. To believe in the Lord Jesus Christ is to keep His commandments in order to abide in His Love. If one believed in Him one should also partake in His supper which is His Body, Blood, Soul and Divinity to have life in Him. On the Eve of His passion Jesus instituted the Holy Eucharist, a Sacramental expression of the Easter Mystery in which He offered His Body and Blood as food instituting at the same time the priesthood. Thereafter, He authorized His Apostles to celebrate this Mystery as often as possible in memory of Him, proclaiming His Death and Resurrection until He comes again. The celebration of the Eucharist is a wonderful beautiful Divine Mystery testifying God's Love for humanity. It is the fulfilment of the above citation of Jesus in Jn 6 vs 53 – 58 confirming life is only attained by eating His Flesh and drinking His Blood. During the Super of the Lamb, Heaven and Earth unite, the Blessed Virgin Mary, St. John the Apostle, St. Mary Magdalene, the Holy Angels and Archangels, and the Saints are present, on Calvary, as the transubstantiation of the Body, Blood, Soul and Divinity of our Lord Jesus Christ takes place during the unbloody Sacrifice of the Lamb of God to the Eternal Father in the Liturgy of the Eucharist. The Priest, who is now Jesus, in that very instance, as He speaks the Words of Jesus Christ on the Eve of His Passion officiates then, though the naked eyes cannot see Him. This is Faith. The heart that loves sees and believes. Religion is Faith. Jesus takes His Sacrifice, the sacrifice of the members of His Mystical Body, all the infirmities, worries, problems, ailments, whatever each of His member came with to the Eucharistic Celebration, unites them with His Sacrifice and offers it all to His Eternal Father in atonement for our sins and the sins of the whole world. The little drop of water into the wine before the consecration represents the members of His Mystical Body. The pilgrim Church here on Earth is united at each Mass with the Church triumphant in Heaven singing the Gloria with the heavenly Angels in praise of the Almighty God. The Eucharistic Christ is food for the soul, from Him the soul is sanctified, nourished and obtains all he needs on his pilgrim journey to his Eternal destination in Heaven with Jesus, for Jesus and in Jesus. The Eucharist is the source and summit of the Christian Faith. The Sacrament of Reconciliation prepares the soul for a worthy communion. This is believing in the Lord Jesus Christ and be saved. This is abiding in His Love. This is keeping His Commandments, to conform with His image and be in union with Him.

Unfortunately, non-Catholics, Evangelist Lutheran Christians and sects receive Communion, not Holy Communion, having taking the words of our Lord symbolically, depriving themselves the union with Jesus Christ. Jesus is not a symbol, He is a Person. Jesus is truly God and truly Man. He is God and He is Alive! Without assimilating the Body, Blood, Soul and Divinity of our Lord Jesus Christ, the Life giving meal of the soul one cannot forge a personal relationship with Him. One cannot have a relationship with a stranger. If one does not have the Holy Trinity living in one, If Jesus does not live in one, how can one have a relationship with Him? The only condition He gave to live in one with His Father is to eat His Flesh and drink His Blood. Besides, having separated themselves from the Apostolic Succession, ministers of the protestant Churches have robbed themselves the authority for the transubstantiation of the bread and wine into the Body, Blood, Soul and Divinity of Jesus Christ. Therefore, being outside the ship, the Church, which Jesus Himself pilots, to live in the assumption communion is a symbol, the ministers of these Churches and sects, knowing fully well they have no authority for the transubstantiation, deceive themselves and their members who follow them blindly. The adherence to false belief and false teaching leads to perdition. The ship will never sink. The Church of Jesus Christ remains until the end of the world just as Jesus said. Jesus did not mean thousands of Churches calling His name, no, He meant the Church He founded "You are Peter and upon this Rock I will build my Church and gate of hell will not prevail against it" This is the Church He means!

Certainly, no one would like to hear on that day "I do not know you" like some of the Jewish exorcists, the sons of Sceva in Ephesus, who, having observed how God did extraordinary miracles by the hands of Paul, so much so that some took his handkerchiefs or apron to the sick and diseases left them, and tried themselves to cast out evil spirits by saying "I adjure you" by the Jesus whom Paul preaches", What did the evil spirit say to them? "Jesus I know, and Paul I know; but who are you?" and the possessed man leapt on them, and overpowered them. That notwithstanding, it is advisable to keep ones focus on Heaven and contemplate the words of Jesus about Eternal life, hence He made no effort to call back the disciples who deserted Him after hearing about eating His flesh, rather He continued to emphasize the necessity of it, turning to the twelve He asked "Will you also go away?" Simon Peter, the spokesman of the apostles, answered "Lord, to whom shall we go? You have the words of eternal Life; and we have believed, and have come to know, that you are the Holy one of God"

From the scripture it is clear the Church founded on Pentecost in Jerusalem, the One, Holy, Catholic and Apostolic Church, remained together breaking bread. This breaking of bread which took place then in the Church with the Holy See, the seat of Peter, in Jerusalem, is the same breaking of bread taking place in the same One, Holy, Catholic and Apostolic Church today, as it was handed down through the apostolic succession. The Holy See, the seat of Peter, is no more in Jerusalem but in Rome at the Vatican. Jesus is God and His is. If the Church He founded on Peter does not exist anymore, after promising gate of hell will not prevail against her, and that he would be with her until the end of the world, then He is not God because God is, His word is. The

Catholic Church has withstood the trials of time, has been existing for over two thousand years. Jesus is God. He is and His Church is. In His Infinite Wisdom He chose to make the center of Christendom in Rome. When the time was ripe, His Supreme Majesty established His Kingdom on Earth in Rome for the worship of the One and only True God, Who is, Who was, and Who is Forever. He got rid of the worship of false gods, of the city where sins from hell travailed, the glory meant for Him, the One and Only True God, given to lifeless objects, as gods. This notorious Rome, the ruler of the world under Satan was destroyed to emerge the seat of God's Kingdom on Earth, the Eternal City, the Holy See, the seat of Peter, Vicar of Jesus Christ on Earth, the center of Christendom, the people of God, the new Israel. Thus the Almighty God underlined His Supremacy. The Pope, Peter, is the visible Head of the Church, a pillar of unity, stability, preventing anarchy, uncertainty and disorder in the absence of our Lord. The Beauty of the Wisdom of the Almighty God lies in the excellency of His perfection far beyond the comprehension of humanity.

With the segregation from the True Vine, the Body of Christ, church has become an article of commodity. Churches are being opened at will, each professing to serve God. Jesus is displeased. What does one expect when His Blessed Body is torn into bits. What thoughtless maneuver, inconsideration, regardless of the feelings of our Lord Jesus, for anyone who professes to serve Him to ignore His commandment "...that they may be one..." to dare break away from His Church to establish another. How could anyone dare use church as professional arena, for economical purposes to boost one's social status, thereby daring to defy the Holy Will of God. One should not forget that the Almighty God who is most merciful is also most just rendering to every one according to his merit. Truth is bitter, it is also life to anyone who accepts her. Therefore, for the salvation of one's soul it would be wise to refrain from intentionally offending God, misleading others to fill one's pocket. A return to the pattern He designed, the way He desires to be worshipped and adored as God, is advisable. In so doing you would save your soul and the souls of your followers from perdition. The Eternal Father who offered His only begotten Son in atonement for the sins of the world, for you would be pleased to show you mercy. One must bear on mind disobedience has consequences. However, it is yet time to appease God penitentially, accept His Divine Mercy, trust in Him, and come back Home to the One, Holy, Catholic and Apostolic Church He established and serve Him there. Know the Catholic Faith, be part of the Magisterium and enjoy the Goodness of God in His Church.

The Religion we profess is a Mystery. It is not a religion of the book as the protestant brothers and sisters presume, indicating salvation to be only on sola scriptura, basing their belief only on the Bible, denying the saving power of the Church which is Jesus Christ Himself. Unfortunately, this belief is wrong. As already quoted, "I am writing these instructions to you so that, If I am delayed, you may know how one ought to behave in the household of God, which is the church of the living God, the pillar and bulwark of the truth." writes St. Paul 1Tim. 3 vs 15. The Church saves and she is the Authority for the Christian Faith. The evangelical brothers do themselves no favor in the belief Catholics do not read the bible. In fact the Catholic Faith is based on the bible and also on tradition. „So then, brethren, stand firm and hold to the traditions which you were taught by us, either by word of mouth or by letter." 2 Thes. 2 vs.15 ‚Ignorance of scripture is ignorance of Christ' The Catholic Mass comprises of two parts, the Liturgy of the word, readings from the Holy scripture to prepare the Faithful for the Liturgy of the Holy Eucharist when the Word Incarnate, Jesus Christ, our Resurrected Lord of Lords, the Royal High Priest who is in Heaven offering Himself to the Eternal Father and through the Power of the Holy Spirit comes to earth to nourish the Faithful with His Resurrected Body under the appearances of Bread and wine so that in assimilating Him we come to know what it means to belong to the Family of God. We come to know Love. God's Love which is a burning Furnace that longs to consume us desperately to enable souls who surrender to Him in humble trust, who receive Him in a state of grace in the Sacrament of His Love, the Holy Eucharist be transformed and conform themselves to the image of Jesus Christ to live with Him eternally in Eternity. In Him is the fullness of the Holy Trinity. How awesome is the Catholic Spirituality. It is worth knowing!

Martin Luther, the revolutionist, being afraid of Purgatory, in his translation of the Bible, removed the books unfavorable to him, such as Maccabees which talks about purgatory, to suit himself. Martin Luther and his counterparts did not favor Jesus by splitting the Church He shed His Most Precious Blood to found, desiring Her so much to "be one as we are one." If Martin Luther's complaint about the Church was generated out of genuine love for God it would not have induced him to segregation. He would have remembered "leave the weeds to grow with the tares, the enemy planted them" Unfortunately, there is no other option than to accept his move was instigated by selfishness and by his fears. How unfortunate, he forgot fears cannot change the Truth of God, rather the Trust in God removes fear. Jesus said "Be not afraid" Nevertheless, Martin Luther was granted sixty days to make his point, rather he chose the broader way of segregation drawing followers with him. In his segregation he removed the key Sacraments which grant sanctifying grace to the soul, the Sacrament of the Eucharist and Penance. Although he believed in the Real Presence of Jesus Christ in the Eucharist, yet he taught his church the opposite doctrine.

If there was no need for the Sacrament of Penance or Reconciliation, it would not have been necessary for Jesus to breath on His Apostles saying "receive the Holy Spirit, whoever sins you forgive are forgiven, the ones you retain are retained". How could Martin Luther and his fellow Reformers, dared, with their reformation and segregation, tamper with the Divine design of Jesus Christ for His Holy Church which He Himself pilots. How could they have dared tear apart the Mystical Body of Christ, which He designed to be one as the Holy Trinity is One.

One begins to wonder if Martin Luther and the Reformers, including the sectarianists who tore from the torn, failed to realize they would not escape the inevitable encounter with God face to face, after their earthly life to account for their disobedience, disorganizing God's institution, before His judgement seat, the judgement seat of the Almighty God.

Now concerning their followers Jesus said "When a blind man leads the blind both will fall into the pit" therefore, the Catholic Church is justified when She says "Those outside the Church without their own fault" may have the chance of eternal salvation. However, it all depends on Our Lord Jesus Christ who knows the secrets of the heart to determine who those are. His Mystical Body, the Church, whose soul is the Holy Spirit will never succumb to the gate of hell. As already mentioned, protestant and sectarian churches emphasize their adherence to the things in the Bible alone, forgetting they owe the compiling of the Bible to the Catholic Church. Besides, with an incomplete Bible as theirs, hence Martin Luther removed some books for his convenient, how could they have the whole Truth. Moreover, by rejecting tradition they fall short of the beauty of the magisterium of the Catholic Church and of the richness of the Christian Faith. Without humility it is impossible to please God. Lack of humility is a source of spiritual blindness. To believe only in the Bible yet blind to the truth which is in the Bible is a tragedy. A visible proof of the true Church, the new Israel of the new Covenant, is the uniformity of Her Liturgies, the Liturgy of the Word and the Liturgy of the Eucharist, the two parts of the Mass, all over the world. In every Roman Catholic Church all over the world every Catholic feels at home. The same Bible reading is read at Mass, in Rome, Asia, Africa, Europe, America, all over the world. The same form of celebrating Mass. Is that not wonderful? It did not matter in what language the Mass is being celebrated every Catholic follows the Mass. One understands what goes on because it is the same thing. This is a sign of Divine manifestation in His One, Holy, Catholic and Apostolic Church whose Soul is the Holy Spirit, the Church of Jesus Christ which He Himself pilots, quite unlike the protestant and sectarian churches who have different rituals and are not united and in some cases envy one another. Humanity is endowed with intellect, with reason to differentiate right from wrong. "Obedience is better than sacrifice."

Thinking of the Magisterium of the Catholic Church, the immense wealth of the teachings of the early Church fathers handed down to the Church through the centuries – the Church triumphant in Heaven, the Holy Angels and Saints, Our Blessed Mother – the Blessed Virgin Mary – Mother of God – our Mother by whom we become brothers and sisters of Jesus Christ, full of Grace, the model of sainthood, who leads every Christian to her Divine Son, one cannot help but wonder how these ministers could deprive themselves and their followers all these overwhelming truths of Divine revelation and yet profess to be ministers of God. The choice of luxury, preference of self-esteem to obedience to God's Holy Will, rejecting the One Holy, Catholic and Apostolic Church, founded by Jesus Himself on Peter and the Apostles, with Her bishops in an unbroken line of apostolic succession, is not without consequence. The Church of God, the One Holy, Catholic and Apostolic Church, enriched with seven Sacraments handed down to Her by Jesus Christ Himself who is the full focus at Mass, especially in the Liturgy of the Eucharist when He is present Body, Blood, Soul and Divinity, as Jesus Christ of Nazareth, Son of God and Son of Virgin Mary, God and Man, the glorified Jesus, the God-Head, is a Eucharistic Church and not a church of the book, therefore She is the one and only true Church, the new Israel of the new covenant. Jesus Christ is fully present in the Holy Eucharist. To receive the Almighty God, Lord of Heaven and Earth should be a compulsion for every Christian in adoration, respect and awe, contemplating the wonder and Beauty of the Highest God. Jesus is the Focus at Mass not the ministers as is the case with the protestant and sects as they do not have the Eucharistic Lord, His real presence. What a big difference!

That notwithstanding, protestants, the Lutheran churches, ordain female pastors, condone and tolerate same sex relationships. They have with the world redefined marriage, whereby same sex pastors live together. What a moral decay! How could one who should oppose such, take the lead to defy God's Law and yet presume to serve the Almighty God who instituted marriage as a Sacrament between a man and a woman? Would such people be able to look God in the eye? Do they not believe any more on the God they serve? What do they take God for? Is their focus on Heaven or on hell? Hopefully, they do believe in hell. Whoever knows to do good and does not do it to him it is sin. Who is man to change the ordinances of God? Does not his intellect make him realize he dare not redefine natural law? How then do the Lutherans, protestants expect to be taken serious about ecumenism? A penitent and a contrite heart, for the segregation from God's Holy Church, for the introduction of female pastors and bishops, would have been the right thing for them to have done. "Let a woman learn in silence with all submissiveness. I permit no woman to teach or to have authority over men; she is to keep silent. For Adam was formed first, then Eve; and Adam was not deceived, but the woman was deceived and became a transgressor" The acceptance of co-habitation of female pastors, homosexual pastors, redefinition of marriage is wrong! Do you really want to come back to your roots? to reunite with the One Holy Catholic and Apostolic Church Jesus instituted? Is lust of great importance to you than your souls? The Lord God is a Holy God. He hates sin. One can only deceive oneself but not God. The Lord knows those who are His. "Let everyone who names the name of the Lord depart from iniquity"

CHAPTER V

POLITICAL DECAY

Humanity is most fortunate to have a most loving and merciful Father. The ocean of His Divine Mercy never dries up. Before He comes again as Judge He shows mercy to everyone. It did not matter if one pleased Him or not, one only needs to appeal to His merciful Heart. As a God of Love and a very compassionate God everyone who calls on His Divine Mercy does not go empty handed, as He hopes at the same time, for the return of everyone to His Divine Will. His Fatherly Love longs for the surrender of His Beloved Children to His Holy Will. All the members of the protestant and sectarian churches – Pentecostal churches – their male and female pastors who indulge in same-sex relationships, are also God's Beloved children and He desires them back, repentantly in humble trust, to His Holy Church, from where they broke away, and be enriched with sanctifying Grace through the reception of the Sacraments He entrusted to His Holy Church in order to prepare themselves to live with Him, for Him and in Him eternally in Heaven. The nature of God is Love. Love is free not forced, therefore, He gave everyone free-will. Jesus taught us God's Will, prayed for us all to abide in His love, to be one with Him as He is one with the Father. The penalty for sin He took upon Himself, reconciled us with God, opened the Gate of Heaven for us and gave us life. Having gone through terrible bodily pain in His humanity for love of us, there is no sin He will not forgive if we repentantly trusted, with love, in His Divine Mercy. He forgives even the worst sinners. Homosexuals, lesbians, criminals, if they turned repentantly in humble trust to Jesus, realizing how deeply they hurt their Heavenly Father who loves them infinitely, with the indulgence in the sins from hell, which He hates like the pest, they will receive Mercy. Those who change the way God made them will also receive Mercy if they repented. His love for you is above your sin, therefore, repent and ask for His assistance to help you overcome your weakness. If you made honest effort, relying on the Grace of your Heavenly Father you would, before you know it be rid of that weakness. It is a big shame and unnatural that a man should marry a man, a woman to marry a woman. It is an abomination, even more, when pastors marry themselves and openly acknowledge their homosexuality. Have they lost sight of Heaven and are prepared to bear the bitter consequence of eternal damnation? To co-exist with the devil and all the demons in hell eternally, what a scare! Nevertheless, there is still time to make hay while the sun shines, stop the sins for which nations ceased to exist. Stop hurting your Father, the God who loves you with infinite love. He wants to save you and give you the Kingdom, but He cannot cease your free-will. Love does not compel, love is a free gift of self in sacrifice.

"The fear of God is the beginning of wisdom" Every level-headed human being, who possesses an iota of the fear of God, should regard with remorse and awe the indifferences shown to the ordinances of the Deity God who holds the world in his Hands, the Lord of Heaven and Earth, that the unnatural has replaced the natural, so much so, that those in authority give a deaf ear to "... render to Caesar the things that are Caesar's and to God the things that are God's." Secularization and materialism has become the tune of the day, everyone dancing to it and politics a skeleton of itself. How disappointing, politicians whose role it is to see to the maintenance of the Divine Law now render to Caesar what belongs to Caesar and what belongs to God. In the cloak of ego, ambition, greed, selfishness, conceit, they hunger for worldly position and power, thereby, fall prey to political decay. Consequently to these drives they become blind to the Divine Will, to the Ordinances of the Creator of the Universe, to the law of nature, passing laws contrary to the law of the Almighty God, challenging the God of Creation by ignoring His design for human existence in this Universe, setting things in their own pattern to suit their sinful mode of life. To introduce laws prohibiting Crosses in certain places such as in the classrooms, courtrooms and public squares is absurd and unrealistic. What a pity, they fail to honor and respect the sign of the redemption of humanity. The Almighty God, Creator of Heaven and Earth, the Supreme Majesty, took the form of a slave, shed His Most precious Blood for this sinful world, for humanity, that we may have life, died for us on the Cross, don't you, politicians, leaders of the nations of this world, think it befitting to at least make it lawful for Crosses to be hung in classrooms, courtrooms and in public squares in honor and respect to such a Good and Merciful God? If the western world is a Christian world, why then should the sign of Christianity be prohibited? How could someone who passes such laws sleep soundly without conscience? Has he lost focus of what it's all about, that on his expiration he must give account to God? To prohibit the Cross, the victorious Cross of our Redeemer, the sign of the Holy Cross of our lord Jesus Christ on which He paid a bitter price for the redemption of humanity is thoughtless and ingratitude in its highest degree. One should not be surprised at the state of events in the world today. The world does not belong to man but to God and He alone has the fate of the world in His Hands, therefore politicians must see themselves compelled to obey God and not man, make a U-turn back to the ordinances of God if their interest is the peace of the world, an end to plagues, wars, terrors and natural catastrophes. God's patience should not be taken for granted.

How shocking and unhealthy for France to pass a law allowing homosexuals the right to marry and adopt children. There is indeed reason for worry as it appears politicians have sold their conscience to Satan hence their encouragement of the sins from hell the abode of Satan and all the evil spirits. Do they think they are being favorable to these homosexuals? No, rather they are assisting them on their journey to perdition. Have they considered life with Satan and his company of evil spirits in hell throughout eternity eternally? Certainly, they cannot expect to be admitted into Heaven if they so willfully topple the commandment of God their Father who has loved them with an infinite love, hurting, thoughtlessly the Most Sacred Heart of Jesus Christ who suffered such bitter passion, shading His Most Precious Blood for love of them. How could they have put a deaf ear to the warnings of the Church and the mass demonstration of the common people who elected them. How could any level-headed human being condone such absurd, nauseating, unnatural, dirty practices as homosexuality, such abominations? Does common sense not get into a fit of revolutionary uproar at the mere mention of it? Homosexuality, same-sex relationship is an ailment of the soul which needs a cure from a specialist for sick souls.

The Specialist for sick souls is God, the Creator of souls. All there is to it is a penitential heart, a return to the most merciful God the Father, who awaits such souls with great love to heal them. How disappointing it is that France, home of the Most Sacred Heart of Jesus, after tasting God's Mercy, would turn round, under a president, Francois Hollande, whose political ambition is more important than the Holy Will of God, and ignore the living evidence of the God of Love and Mercy present everywhere in his country, to turn round to practice the very sins for which God the Son sacrificed Himself on the Cross, the very sins for which nations, such as Sodom and Gomorrah, seized to exist. Has France forgotten her heritage? Has she forgotten the demonstration of the power of the Almighty God through the many Saints God raised up among the French? The disregard of the Holy Will of God has its consequences, at least history bears witness to it.

Furthermore, it is heart-rending to hear Ireland joined the chorus, legalizing abortion, despite the mass demonstration for life. Irish politicians ignored, like France, their patron Saint, St. Patrick and the Divine Favor granted them at Noack, the visit of the blessed Virgin Mary, St. Joseph, St. John and the Lamb representing Jesus Christ, the Lamb of God in the Eucharist. The Shrine of this apparition is still present in Ireland at

Noack, an attraction for pilgrims. Do you politicians think the Almighty God who created the whole Universe and you, cannot handle what is His? The pregnant women, you say, might be in danger of death, is the Almighty Father not their Father? Do you think He does not realize the state of those women? Did God ask you to help Him decide who should live and who should not? What if the woman dies in child birth, what about it? Do you not realize God can save the life of both mother and child, if He wants, even when doctors might give them no chance of surviving? Why do you choose to interfere with God's Divine plan?

Heaven and earth and all in them are God's, they belong to Him. It is His Divine Right to do what He wants with what is His, including with you because He created you and you belong to Him. All humanity belongs to the Almighty God and for every individual He created He has a unique plan. No one can function without Him. Everyone is living on borrowed time. Everyone is what he is because God wills it so. Do not grow wings because you have intelligence, knowledge or wisdom. It is not your credit but God's Divine Mercy and Grace for a purpose to which you must account for before His judgement Throne. Therefore, your life is not yours it belongs to God who created you, loves you and desires you to inherit Heaven. Bear on mind that every law you passed in this world contrary to the Holy Will of God you must be accountable for it, therefore think twice before daring to challenge God. Obey God and live!

One cannot help but wonder at what Europe has become. Has Europe sold her conscience in pursuit of materialism and selfish ambition? Most unfortunate it appears she has. This was a continent of hope, endowed with Divine Graces, adorned like a bride for her Bridegroom, and blessed with so many great Saints. A continent, like a flower blossoming from its buds, portraying the beauty, splendor and greatness of the Almighty God which led to her resurrection from barbarism to civilization through Christianity. It is sad to observe the course of events in Europe, how fast she has piloted herself into paganism, locking her Christian norms in the drawer, and dancing to the tune of hell, encouraging and indulging in secularism, abortion, same sex marriage, Euthanasia. How she strives at infringing the rights of the Catholic Church Who is her Benefactor, thereby challenging the Supreme Authority of the Almighty God, Jesus Christ, the Founder of the Catholic Church. The legalization of sins as norms of good behavior against the natural Laws of the Creator, imposing the acceptance of such laws from the pit of hell on the Catholic Church, is definitely an offense against our Lord Jesus Christ Who will not remain a silent Observer for long as He promised to be with His Church till the end of time. To dare to tamper with religious liberty in the pretext of political wisdom is nothing but lack of insight. Wisdom is the recognition of Divine Providence, accepting the Ordinances of God and keeping them. Most important is wisdom the recognition of the sacrifice of the only Begotten Son of God, Jesus Christ, on the Cross, appreciating it and having Heaven in focus, trusting and hoping in Jesus Christ, observing His Precepts with the aim to please Him and make Heaven. One thing Europe must bear on mind is that God is her strength and not European union, without God European union has no future. Europe should cease offending God. If European Union wants to survive, then she must turn back to God, consecrate herself to the Sacred Heart of Jesus Christ who has loved her tenderly and shown her great Mercy. Europe should console the Sacred Heart of Jesus from whose Goodness she has so richly benefited.

The pursuit of wealth and fame at the risk of eternal life with God in Heaven is complete foolishness, blindness with deepest consequence. Heaven is real and hell is real. Although it is not Gods Holy Will anyone should perish in hell, yet a great number of people are steering themselves into that destination on their own free-will. Jesus the good Shepherd, a Most Loving God, is continuously pleading with Love for all hearts to turn to Him Who is their Father. This world is transitory, ephemeral, it would be destroyed by fire and the Lord will make all things new. Seek therefore, the God of Love whose merciful Heart is wide open for every sinner while it is yet day, render to Him what is His before He comes as a righteous Judge. A word is enough for the wise. Humility is of God, pride is Satanic, choose life not death.

Whenever the slogan "yes we can" is heard one cannot help but remembering its origin, the slogan that catapulted Barack Obama, to the status of president, thus, making him the first Afro-American president of the United States of America, the president of the most powerful nation in the world. His choice as president was certainly seen as beneficial to humanity, in it's significant for overcoming racial discrimination, a sign of hope for the less privileged, regardless of color and origin. One who would turn round the world economy to its balance, a new leadership for a better world. However, despite his second term in office he has not been able to meet up with what was expected of him.

There is no course for surprise because when the consciousness of the higher power governing the universe is lost, the Divine Will of the Creator ignored, self-esteem culminates into the lacking of the fear of God, embedded in political ambition, egoism and selfishness undermine primary concern, conscience disappears then evil is promoted. When one assumes to know how to run the world, which he did not create, better than Him Who created it, one tends to precipitate into being the instrument of Satan, the enemy of God, the Creator, by whom all things exist. How could one who calls himself a Christian condone all that Christianity is against. How could a Christian be an impediment to Christian liberty, paying no heed to the constitution of the fathers of America who set religious liberty as a pillar for the existence of the American people.

Furthermore, how absurd and baffling it is that a Christian president should be in support of same-sex marriage, encouraging homosexuality and lesbianism, without any consideration of the ultimate consequence it could have for his soul, deliberately hurting the Most Sacred Heart of the God who created Him.

One cannot help but admire the courage of Russia, who under communism, promoted atheism, to denounce homosexuality, disallowing even the mention of it in their country for the moral upbringing of their children. At least the western countries should learn from their Russian counterparts, yet, bearing on mind Putin's camouflage, as he is a green snake in a green grass, who would stop at nothing for his political ambition. It is simply not right for any country to use either her economic strength or military strength to ride over another country less favored, without taking into consideration the feeling of the God of Creation who granted everyone freedom of existence, therefore, nobody has the right to cease another's freedom. If only the governing authorities would realize the system of this world is transitory, the politicians piping for a while and are heard no more, that someday, they would be gone to give an account of their life to Him Who gave it to them, then they would be less in pursuit of worldly prestige but rather more concerned about the well-being of their subjects in accordance to the precepts of God.

This is the fate of existence in this terrible wilderness, the world which Satan polluted, a world waiting for her ultimate destruction for a better world of peace and love. Nevertheless, the world would be a better place if everyone would keep focus on Heaven, contemplate on eternal Joy and life everlasting, how to achieve it and not deliberately reaching out for eternal damnation. This would awaken the fear of God, the search for Him, who would make Himself known, Jesus Christ, the Merciful Loving Good God who is waiting patiently, tenderly, for His estranged Children to come Home into His Arms.

However, it was surprising to see the excitement with which Barack Obama received the news of the legalization of same sex marriage, as he was to board the plane, on his way to his African trip. One may wonder if he forgot he is a father who owes his daughters and his grandchildren, the observation of natural laws in a healthy world, according to the Holy Will of the Creator who called the world into existence. To God, he definitely owes obedience and must render to Him an account of his presidency which God assigned to him. He must realize it is God who put him in that position for a purpose and not for him to encourage all that God is against. In all things God comes first before anyone else. Every Christian should be aware of this. Humanity must be aware the Almighty God, in His infinite Goodness and Mercy, provided them with His commandments for a peaceful co-existence therefore, these commandments should be observed with respect and awe of the Creator, in gratitude to Him Who is their loving Father. "Do you not know that the unrighteous will not inherit the kingdom of God? Do not be deceived; neither the immoral, nor idolaters, nor adulterers, nor homosexuals, nor thieves, nor the greedy, nor drunkards, nor revilers, nor robbers will inherit the kingdom of God" Intimate relationship reserved for male and female in marital union is an ordinance, a sacrament instituted by God Himself, no created being has the right to change it. Moreover, to legalize such sinful abnormal behavior is to encourage those who indulge in such acts on their pitiable journey into eternal damnation. The Almighty God to whom humanity owes their existence is the Supreme Authority whose Commandments must be regarded by all as priority and the observance of them should be seen as an obligation.

The God of Love who in His infinite Goodness is no respecter of persons, cannot, would not and did not create any one with the inclination to same sex relationships when He Himself is against such. Anyone with the inclination of homosexuality or lesbianism has simply a weak will. Such persons live on lame excuses it is not their fault, they are born that way. They are wrong! That is an understatement and an insult to the God Who is Love, Who created humanity, out of His Divine Mercy. Be it known that the God Who has a Merciful Love for humanity, could simply not create any one with same-sex attraction, when such is a sin, a mortal sin that offends Him. Besides, the human race is His Beloved Children whom He loves equally and infinitely. For them He shades tears of sorrow thirsting for their love with a burning desire to see them in Heaven. A God who is in agony for such Children who would eventually end up in hell could not possibly have created them with such abnormality for hell. It makes no sense. That would be contradictory to the nature of God Who is Love. It is no use to deceive oneself with the notion one cannot do anything about it, of course one can. Everyone is created with intellect and knows good and bad. All it takes is a strong will. One must develop an honest desire to get rid of it by looking at it in its ugliness, see how nauseating such practices are and call a spade a spade. Same sex relationship is a mortal sin. Anyone inclined to such should seek to obtain Grace from God in humbleness of heart, repentantly. The God, our Father, in the ocean of His Divine Mercy, would be happy to grant this Grace to set the soul free from such deadly bondage in which Satan, the shameless enemy of humanity has placed him.

Everyone should be what God created him to be. God created everyone for a purpose. Better be maimed and enter into the Kingdom of Heaven than enjoy the unfulfilling lustful pleasures of this transient world offered deceitfully, on golden plates, by the enemy of the Holy Cross of salvation, to souls who are weak, on their own accord simply due to their unwillingness to be vigilant, to be aware of Satan's craftiness, consequently steering themselves to the ultimate perdition. Hell is a reality. It is not a place for any level headed person. Open up your heart to your Heavenly Father who has promised you Eternal Salvation in Heaven and be consoled in His fatherly Love. He is yearning for your love. Give Him your heart, unite your will with His, trust in Him, then He will, in due time, gradually transform you to understand love, reveal Himself to you and you will find peace.

That notwithstanding, any pretense of ignorance of the Divine ordinances of God is irresponsibility and disloyalty to our Lord. Did the

Almighty God, in His Infinite Wisdom, not reveal the incarnation of His Divine Son through His prophets long before this took place? At the fullness of time, Jesus, the only begotten Son of God, took flesh. Everything foretold about Him were fulfilled in Him to the last letter. His Humanity and Divinity were portrayed in the life He lived. He wept, toiled, and mourned, characteristics of humanity. His capability to perform miracles, such as healing the sick, make the lame walk, the deaf to hear, those possessed with evil spirits to be whole, His capability to walk on water, to forgive sins, to turn water to wine and His command over nature proved His Divinity. While He was asleep, during the storm, His apostles woke Him up "Master, do you not care that we perish?" Jesus rebuked the storm "peace be still" The storm obeyed Him. Only God can forgive sin, command nature, change the nature of one substance into another because He created them. God alone can do the things He did. Jesus is God. God is Love not violence as some religions demonstrate. Bearing on mind Buddha, Mohamed, and other religious founders came after Jesus Christ, they neither taught with authority, as Jesus did, nor performed miracles. Jesus conquered death with His glorious resurrection because He is God.

If Jesus was merely a prophet, then He must have been a prophet after the heart of God. God must have been pleased with Him to have made Him the only prophet to whom He endowed with such great power which only Himself possess, which was lacking in the other prophets who came after Him. Therefore, if Jesus pleased God to such extent to have obtained such favors from Him, then Jesus must be believed so as to please God who sent Him. As for the other prophets who came after Jesus, there was no one sent to prepare the way for their coming as was with the case of Jesus Christ. John the Baptist came to prepare the way for the coming of Jesus Christ. Jesus Christ alone taught with authority, as the Son of God. These reasons should infuse in one the fear of God and a search for the truth. With this indisputable truth, therefore, to deny that Jesus Christ came in the flesh is to deny the salvation He won for mankind, thereby separating one-self from Eternal Life with Him in Eternity. The same fate awaits all those who engage in abnormal mode of life, supporting and encouraging abortion, homosexuality, sexual laxity, all kinds of immorality, if repentance is not realized before life expires. It is indeed a pity for anyone to undergo operation to change his sex contrary to the design of his Creator. One cannot simply, for his lust, dare challenge his Creator without His permission. It is better to remain the way God created you. Do you not realize O man you do not own yourself and must give an account to your Creator before His judgement seat someday when He requires your soul? Humanity is most fortunate to have a God Who is Love, Good, Merciful and Kind, Who offers to everyone reasonable opportunity for a change, coupled with His Divine assistance, if only He is given the chance. However, everyone enjoys his free-will to seek to know God, love Him, and keep His Precepts, which are easy for those who love Him. Nevertheless, the choice for hell or Heaven, depends on the choice one makes here on earth, on one's free-will. God desires everyone in Heaven. Don't miss the opportunity!

"For the wrath of God is revealed from heaven against all ungodliness and wickedness of men who by their wickedness suppress the truth. For what can be known about God is plain to them, because God has shown it to them. Ever since the creation of the world his invisible nature, namely, his eternal power and deity, has been clearly perceived in the things that have been made. So they are without excuse; for although they knew God they did not honor him as God or give thanks to him, but they became futile in their thinking and their senseless minds were darkened. Claiming to be wise, they became fools, and exchanged the glory of the immortal God for images resembling mortal man or birds or animals or reptiles. Therefore God gave them up in the lusts of their hearts to impurity, to dishonoring of their bodies among themselves, because they exchanged the truth about God for a lie and worshiped and served the creature rather than the creator, who is blessed forever!

Amen. For this reason God gave them up to dishonorable passions. Their women exchange natural relations for unnatural, and the men likewise gave up natural relations with women and were consumed with passion for one another, men committing shameless acts with men and receiving in their own persons the penalty due for their error." Whoever has ears to hear let him hear.

It is astonishing and disappointing that Britain, who should have known better as history reveals, due to her role in persecuting the mystical body of Jesus Christ during the reign of king Henry the eighth, failed to be an example to the other European nations by fighting strongly against evil in the hope of appeasing the Almighty Father who is being continually offended by the rampant evil in the world. For Britain to encourage same sex marriage is an abomination, a defiance to the Almighty God. For this abominations to be endorsed with the signature of queen Elizabeth II is an insult, an offence to the Supreme Divine Majesty Himself. How could Britain, a Christian country with a past, dare to interfere with Divine Law. Should this gesture of the queen be taken as a challenge to the patience of His Divine Majesty, the God of Creation?

One would have expected repentance, reparation and atonement for the sins of segregation from the Mystical Body of Christ, the banning of the Roman Catholic Church, an attempt to eradicate the Catholic Faith in England by Henry VIII in defiant of the Pope, the persecution of Catholics in general which was propagated by Elizabeth I after the reign of her father Henry VIII. How wonderful it would have been had the queen of England, Elizabeth II apologized for the wrong done by her predecessors to Jesus Christ by persecuting Him in His One, Holy, Catholic and Apostolic Church, and be converted to the Catholic Faith. A penitential gesture that would have set an example to her subjects, the British people and appeased His Supreme Majesty. It should be clear God is not a respecter of persons, although Merciful, He is also a just God. Therefore, it is profitable to benefit from His Divine Mercy than face His Justice. Sometimes, one is favored with long life for a purpose, but there are those who do not utilize this favor to work out their salvation. Separation from the Church of Jesus Christ is separation from Him. Church does save. The true Church, the One, Holy, Catholic and Apostolic Church founded by Jesus saves. In Her is the fullness of the Truth and to Her is given authority from above, through the Apostolic Succession to spread the Gospel of Jesus Christ. She is in possession of all the Sacraments from which sanctifying grace is bestowed. There is no shame in saving one's soul from damnation. The kingdoms of this world are transitory. It would be a pity to swim in wealth and pomp in this world and end up in hell. There is everlasting fire, eternal damnation, no wealth and no pomp. Therefore, make hay while the sun shines. There is no shame in Humility for Eternal life with Jesus in Eternity. After all, Jesus Christ Himself to whom Heaven and Earth belong, the Owner of Wealth and Luxury, humbled Himself and took flesh, became poor to make us rich, what is man that he would not humble himself for a life with Jesus, in Jesus, for Jesus in Eternity? For a life with Jesus Eternally in Heaven no sacrifice is too much.

It never rains but it purrs. England, although not yet recovered from her offence against Jesus Christ by persecuting Him through her King Henry VIII, in His Mystical Body the Church, now dares to go against His Divine Law, encouraging the sins from hell which caused Sodom and Gomorrah vanish from the surface of the Earth. "Saul, Saul, why are you persecuting me?" "Who are you Lord?" "I am Jesus Christ whom you are persecuting" Thus Jesus Christ Himself testified His Church is Himself. However, Saul became Paul, a great Apostle, repented of his blindness and ignorance of the scripture in his zeal for God, recognized God's Merciful Love for him and was conquered. Being now instigated, he emptied out himself for the Mystical Body of the most loving God, Who emptied Himself out for him, suffering terrible physical, mental agonizing torture, even death on the Cross, for love of him. But Henry VIII, on the contrary, broke away from the pope, made himself head of the English church, paved way for other pieces to segregate from his piece and so helped to tear apart the Mystical Body of Jesus Christ. Now instead of engaging herself for a reconciliation with Rome – the Vatican, Britain continues to defy the Holy Will of God paying no attention to the grievous consequence, ignoring deliberately, the Divine Supremacy of the Almighty God could cause her. One should not take God's patience for granted. Heaven helps those who help themselves. If only England would reach out her hand to God Who is tenderly stretching out His Hand to pull her out from her sinking boat into His Boat that never sinks, her beauty would be illuminated beyond her expectation. Is going against God's Holy Will your way to express gratitude to the Almighty God Who took Flesh to reconcile you with Himself by shading His Most Precious Blood to free you from death for you to share His Divine Life with Him in Heaven? Remember, the kingship or queenship of this world and any reputable worldly position ends in this world. They are transitory. The Almighty Father weeps and yearns for you to return to Him as His loving obedient Children therefore, do not delay. Give your heart to Jesus who is calling you tenderly now, like a beggar, while it is yet day, before darkness falls. Britain is it not high time you returned to your roots, to your Christian glory before you deviated to the enemy by Henry VIII?

However, it must be emphasized, those who support abnormal mode of life are supporting Satan, defying the Divine set up, and dictating to the Almighty God how His free gift of life should be spent, therefore, are liable to the same consequence of perdition, the goal of those who indulge in it. To participate in sharing stolen goods with a thief, knowing fully well the goods are stolen, makes one a culprit. A spade is a spade.

Therefore, all politicians and judges who support and enforce laws in favor of abortion, promote homosexuality and lesbianism, granting them the right to adopt children contrary to the Holy Will of God who designed marriage between man and woman to parent children, defying with their free-will and clear conscience the Divine Ordinances of God, are liable to Divine wrath. Do you not realize your positions as ruling authorities are not of your own accord, but of Gods Holy Will to maintain law and order and not to serve Satan and become his instruments for poisoning God's children with the sins from hell. "Let every person be subject to the governing authorities. For there is no authority except from God, and those that exist have been instituted by God. Therefore, he who resists the authorities resists what God has appointed, and those who resist will incur judgment. For rulers are not a terror to good conduct, but to bad. Would you have no fear of him who is in authority? Then do what is good, and you will receive approval, for he is Gods servant for your good. But if you do wrong, be afraid, for he does not bear the sword in vain; he is a servant of God to execute his wrath on the wrong doer. Therefore, one must be subject, not only to avoid Gods wrath but also for the sake of good conscience" Ask yourselves you who are in authority if you are terrors to good conduct or to bad. Is God pleased with you?

Now, the governing authorities should not dare defy Gods commandment except of course if they are ready for the consequence. You have failed woefully. How could you dare hurt the Most Sacred Heart of Jesus who has loved you with such infinite Love. Do you not realize you encourage the sins from hell for which He shed His Most Precious Blood for your salvation? Why would you sell your conscience to Satan? Why would you choose death and not Life? Do you not realize you are children of God? Must you sell your souls to Satan for worldly possession, for pomp, pleasures and riches of this transitory world even for perdition? Why are you fighting against God, denying religious liberty, encouraging same sex marriage, abortion, Euthanasia and the like? Why are you trying Gods patience? It is foolishness to take Gods Divine Mercy for granted. Do not call Gods wrath upon yourselves. Do you not know the fear of God is the beginning of wisdom?

All you homosexuals and lesbians rejoicing to have gained the right to enjoy the sins from hell why do you not shut your eyes for a moment and contemplate your life with Satan in hell in eternity eternally? Do not deceive yourselves, there is nothing one cannot overcome if the intension is genuine. Divine Assistance is always lovingly available if sought penitentially in humility. Besides, God created man in His own Image, therefore, that part of God in man, if one is compliant, sustains one from being without conscience, from the state of inability to the state of being able to detect evil. Do not be wise in your own conceit, make a U – Turn and embrace the Divine Mercy of God while you can. "Submit yourselves therefore to God. Resist the devil and he will flee from you. Draw near to God and he will draw near to you. Cleanse your hands, you sinners, and purify your hearts, you men of double mind. Be wretched and mourn and weep. Let your laughter be turned to mourning and your joy to dejection. Humble yourselves before the Lord and he will exalt you" God loves you, He did not create you lesbian or homosexual, it is simply the choice you made allowing Satan deceive you. God is a Most Merciful Father, give your heart to Him, not to Satan, you will discover how fast you would be cured of your ailment. All you need do is trust in Him, accept His Divine Mercy which rules His Justice. To reject His Divine Mercy means your free choice of perdition which you would desperately regret when you behold this Wonderful Merciful God Who is your Father face to face, then there would be no longer mercy. Now is the time to seek His mercy when He is ready to receive you, His prodigal son, in His Arms.

It is indeed praiseworthy for the president of Nigeria, Jonathan, and the Nigerian government as a whole to have taken the lead to condemn evil and passed law against those who practice same sex relationships and those who encourage it. Common sense alone makes one know the absurdity of such abnormal relationships contrary to nature. Therefore, it is advisable for other nations to follow this example to help make the world a better place in order to eradicate evil completely from the surface of the earth, trusting in the Most Precious Blood of Jesus to appease the Almighty Father, while awaiting the second coming of Jesus Christ our Most Faithful and Trustworthy Redeemer, the Prince of peace.

O Father mine Most Divine, how I love Thee.
With infinite Love Your Beloved Children you
adorn, though estranged from You they be,
A shield for them Your Holy Wings be. Alas!
dearest Dad, Most Beloved, tears of worry,
worries untold run down Your Blessed Checks,
Tears of unrequited love they be, sweet Dad,
so much love for estranged children Thine.
Were I but not so little Dad mine, how gladly
would I have brought back to You all estranged
children Thine. How proud your little girl is of You

O Father mine, Most Divine, how I love Thee!
What worries over estranged children Thine
cause You, sweet Dad mine, so Divine, that
Lamentation a welcomed companion mine doth
become. O dear brothers and sisters mine, where
has conscience gone that heart cold doth become.

O how patiently Dad so Divine, doth await your return.
O estranged brothers and sisters mine, into the Arms
of your Father return, Life Eternal from Dad so Divine
embrace, Damnation flee. O Most Beloved Dad mine,
your little girls Wonderful Dad, her pride always remain.

If only Catholic politicians like Joe Biden, not only in the United States of America, but all over the world could practice their Catholic Faith without fear, trusting in the Lord Jesus Christ Who is their Divine Master, a lot of evil would have been prevented in this world. The enemy, Satan would not have had it easy to invade humanity introducing sins from hell. You would have helped save many souls to the joy of the Almighty Father Who would richly reward you in Heaven. Do not be the Pharisees of today giving God lip-service. "Now you Pharisees cleanse the outside of the cup and of the dish, but inside you are full of extortion and wickedness" Has worldly position and political benefits been deeply rooted in you as to forget your focus and the hope of eternal life with Jesus? You modern Pharisees must not forget, if you denied Jesus He would also deny you before His Father. You are supposed to be the light in the darkness of political arena, placing your light on a shelf thereby illuminating your surroundings with a touch on the conscience of your counterparts who are on the verge of perdition. It is your role as Catholic Christians to be a reflection of Jesus Christ in your lives not to dance to the tune of a sick world. You are to carry your Cross and follow Christ, even at the risk of losing your political career or your life for the love of Jesus, as did St. Thomas More, to regain it eternally in Eternity. This is the hope of every Catholic Christian who abides in the Love of God, observing His Commandments with focus on Heaven which is His ultimate goal.

CHAPTER VI

LITTLE SOULS

It is utmost astonishing, indeed most pitiable, the manner in which humanity drifts around, nonchalantly, in this planet Earth in which man is in exile to get to know, love and serve God and then come back to Him in Heaven. This nonchalant attitude of man, who is endowed with the Spirit of God, his origin, is a dangerous game of fate, as man would someday give an account of how he spent his life, on Earth, to the Almighty God Who created him. The failure to realize man's true identity, the reality man originated from God and eventually would go back to Him, is the root of all the problems man faces on the Earth. This nonchalant attitude paves way to man's indifference to the commandments of God, his Creator, which leads to his precipitation into dishonoring the Precious Blood of Jesus Christ, the price of his redemption. Man's selfish dependent on his ego, denial of the existence of God, failure to realize he is nothing without God, leads to his ultimate destruction. Unless man turns to God there would be no peace for him, but conflicts and rivalries. Therefore, to be in harmony with his Creator he must hate sin, nurture the awareness and fear of God. Having been created by a loving Creator, God of Love, Who in His infinite Goodness created him in His own Image and likeness, endowed him with intellect, to enable him, by surveying his environment, he may discover Him in His Creation. Consequently he may become aware of God's existence and seek Him. The Almighty God is always ready to reveal Himself to anyone who sincerely seeks Him. God is a very compassionate Father Who loves with a motherly love and faithful forever. There is nothing He would not do for His children. The trouble is in man not in God who is perfect, faithful and trustworthy. He desires the security of His children.

Every action of God is Love. As children, there is the need to know the Father, keep His precepts to enjoy His Love. He despises sin, therefore, to get along with Him one should honestly desire to avoid sin. Should there be a set back, like the prodigal son, with genuine repentance, for having offended a loving Father, submit to His Divine Mercy in humble trust. The Mercy of God rules His Judgement. What a Most Merciful God our good Lord is.

The human nature, having been stained with original sin, needs transformation to be in conformity with the nature of God who desires man to share in His Divine Life. Therefore, man must surrender completely to the Holy Will of the Almighty God, in Jesus Christ, the only begotten Son of the Eternal Father who offered Himself in sacrifice for the salvation of humanity, for the transformation of man's sinful nature, for eternal life with Him eternally, in Heaven. For this goal, Jesus provided the pilgrim Church with seven Sacraments for Her heavenly bound Eternal Destination.

"A thing of beauty is joy forever" said Shakespeare. How right he was. God is Beauty. There is nothing beautiful but God. God is Beauty, Eternal Joy. From Him creation receives her beauty. It is commonly known like terms beget like terms, so God being Beauty, created souls beautiful, as they are part of Him, loving beautiful children of the Father Who provided them with bodies in which they dwell. Sin therefore, darkens the soul, makes him ugly and evil, otherwise, the original condition of the soul is beauty and love. God the Father is Love. A return of the soul to his original state is the worry of the Almighty Father Who desires every soul to return to his original beauty and nature, inherit the Kingdom and live with Him eternally in Eternity in Heaven. If only the soul would have a glimpse of the heavenly Kingdom no amount of difficulties in this exile would be too much. All that is needed is trust in the Almighty God, in Jesus Christ, patiently keeping the focus on Heaven while drawing strength and courage from His Holy Cross and in His promises. He is Faithful.

What a wonderful delight to be favored by God. In His infinite goodness, endowed with Divine grace, I found myself, just as I lay down to sleep, enveloped by Divine Love. Being in complete surrender to Divine union, totally in ecstasy, drowned in wonder and admiration of God's Beauty, I floated in God as though I was in space, without gravity. How wonderfully Beautiful our good God is. This undeserved grace is nothing to all that He actually is, but enough to fascinate and captivate me leaving me with no words to describe this beautiful wonderful experience. In fact it is best described by personal experience, as there is no word to do justice to such Beauty. To be in this exile Earth and yet out of it, fully aware of my surroundings, in delightful union with God, floating in the bright lighted Space, fully awake in my four walls, leaves me dumbfounded. It was indeed a marvelous, indescribable experience. God is indeed Almighty, a Wonderful Father Who has won all my admiration for Who He is. There will never be true happiness for man unless one opens up to God. He is humanity's Destiny. Human being is a wonderer on Earth searching for his identity. God is his identity. God is his Father. He came from Him and he must someday go back to Him when his time in this exile is up, either to eternal joy in Heaven or to perdition. It all depends on the choice one makes. Man has his destiny in his own hand. If one opens up to God, then He helps one come to the realization of one's true self. All it takes is trust and will to discover this Great Wonderful Loving God humanity has as Father and realize what one has been missing by being estranged to Him.

We are little souls, God's little children, in the enclosure of our bodies. How the Father lavishes the soul with so much love and affection while the soul perches on the Father with delight. My soul magnifies the Lord, for the grace granted me, a poor wretched creature, less than half of an Ant, to have this marvelous experience. We are little beautiful souls of the Eternal Father, ever young, only the human body grows old, but the soul remains radiant, beautiful and little. If only humanity would realize the Supremacy of our God, His Most Majestic Being and give

Him, who humbled Himself that we should call Him "Abba Father", all the honor and glory that He deserves, all respect and awe in deepest humility His glorious reign on earth would be hastened. He has won my admiration and respect. He is a wonderful Father, indeed the best Father, Who only needs to say and it is. He is the God He says He is Who should be loved and feared. His Goodness and Mercy should not be taken for granted. No one knows the creation better than the Creator therefore, it is only by surrendering to the Creator will we begin to get closer to our Creator, to Our God, Our Father, in Jesus Christ, only then are we really on that perfect journey to perfect happiness eternally in Eternity with our Beloved Heavenly Father. Then will we all be looking forward, with excitement, as I do, to that perfect happiness eternally in Eternity with Jesus. To be forever united with my Heavenly Dad, with my Beloved Jesus Christ eternally in Heaven is the secret yearning of my heart. I hope yours too. Now is the time for a decision. Our Beloved Jesus is waiting anxiously to lead us to our Beloved Heavenly Father, Who loves us infinitely. We should not delay. Jesus is knocking on the door of your heart, why not let Him in?

What am I but a little soul, the Father's little girl, His little Mary of the Most Sacred Heart of Jesus, His darling daughter. I simply cannot fathom my fortune, that I am the child of God. In fact the awareness the Almighty God, the living God who created Heaven and Earth and all that is, is my Father, overwhelms me. He is yours too, if you accept Him. O What a fortune! What a relief to entrust myself completely into His fatherly care like a baby in its mother's arms. Interestingly, I discovered that in so doing I lost nothing but rather swim in the ocean of the heavenly Father's Love and care in the beautifully loving warm embrace of my sweet Beloved Jesus, while seeing to His Precepts, which are easy for those who love Him, He grants me the Grace to persevere. Jesus said "be not afraid" The trust in the Lord Jesus Christ and the hope for Heaven earns one the motivation and the Grace to persevere against all the wiles and trials of the enemy. Jesus is faithful, and trustworthy. He is what He said He is.

Heaven is real. Hell is real, as real as you are real, if you do not believe, you will believe when you get there, then it will be too late for a return to God. Humanity is hungry for happiness, spelt in the euphoria the German folk felt for winning the football world championship 2006 and 2014. But such happiness is transient, empty without promise because it is not rooted in God. Without God we are incapable of doing anything, not even the minutest thing such as combing the hair. We are conceited and tend to forget every achievement or success is because God willed it. Therefore, whatever achievement or success the glory belongs to God. Although the euphoria derived in the football world championship is transient, yet it would have been in place to have given God, Who was the key to the successes, the glory. There is always the necessity to thank Him in every condition, for, as a loving Father every Act of His is Love. One may not understand at the moment, but He will make it plain at the right time. Sure one would want such euphoria to last forever, but nothing in this world is forever, at the most a week or more and everything goes back to the original state of boredom, hectic, loneliness, depression and the like. God is Eternal Happiness. God alone is forever. Accepting and reciprocating His Love is a guarantee for Eternal Joy, for Eternal Life in Eternity. Jesus is the answer to man's quest for happiness. If His Love is reciprocated one would discover, on the long run, His Precepts are not difficult to keep. Love bears everything. Harden not your heart against your loving Redeemer, Jesus Christ, for Eternal Happiness. For Heaven, our Father's Kingdom, no suffering is too much.

Bearing on mind we are little souls, existing to know, serve and love God, who are created out of His merciful love, to partake in His Divine Life, we should therefore, especially Catholics, who are in the One, Holy, Catholic and Apostolic Church founded by Jesus, in possession of the whole Truth and all the Sacraments for the sanctification of the soul, aim at living a life worthy of Christ by practicing our Catholic Faith. None Catholics, however, as has been stated earlier, should retrace their steps back to the One, Holy, Catholic and apostolic Church, the Body of Christ, which is their root, for which He shed His precious Blood, desired Her to be one as He is one with His Father. One God, one Faith, one Baptism. Nevertheless, being in the One, Holy, Catholic, and Apostolic Church, without practicing the Catholic Faith, does not guarantee salvation for every Catholic, hence each individual is responsible for his salvation, but he has a better chance due to the fullness of the Truth which the Church possesses and the Sacraments. As the Church is the mystical Body of Christ, therefore She saves, quite unlike the assumption of protestant churches "Church does not save" But of course Church saves, the One, Holy Catholic and Apostolic Church founded by Jesus Christ on Peter saves, because She is Jesus Christ, She is His Body. Besides, Jesus left Her with a promise, gate of hell will not prevail against Her. Jesus is God and when God says, it is. There is no need beating about the bush, the Roman Catholic Church saves! She is Jesus!

If someone loves someone that someone automatically seeks and protects the interest of that someone whom that someone loves. This is exactly my unceasing aim being in love with God. The joy of loving Him compels me to protect His interest regardless of any opposition I might encounter in the course of it. With God's love in my heart the desires of His Most Sacred Heart becomes automatically mine. I have love for every individual which makes it impossible for me to turn the other way and pretend I did not notice anything being done by someone that is contrary to His Holy Will, be it a priest, a laity, or whoever, without politely drawing the attention of whoever that might be, to his wrong doing. Such is an act of love for one's neighbor. He is God's Child and God wants him in Heaven. Jesus desires every soul in Heaven therefore, for the love of Jesus I also do. I have a great yearning to convert sinners, to make atheists realize we have such a wonderful loving God Who is our Father, Who wants all His Children to make Heaven. Loving God compels me to love all He loves and hate all He hates. Due to His infinite Goodness and Mercy I have grown to realize how sad God is and my heart burns with the yearning to console Him. Jesus yearns desperately for man's heart as His tabernacle of consolation. One should not hesitate to co-operate with him nor be afraid, simply trust in Him, He will assist you to love Him.

On one occasion however, after Mass, in the attempt to draw attention of some sisters who dressed indecently, in sexy-outfit, Jesus was not pleased with them in such clothing, they hurt His Sacred Heart, I was met with repulsion. Knowing how distasteful it all was for Jesus, as He watched them approach Him, without conscience, to receive Him in the Holy Eucharist, the Sacrament of His Love, without reverence and awe, my heart reached out to Him in sympathy. I was deeply affected, the tears from His beautiful loving eyes ran down my cheeks, who for our sakes was stripped naked at the scourging, at the crowning with thorns and before the crowd for the crucifixion, all for love of us. How very little do some of us Catholics realize the discomfort Jesus experiences in the hearts that receive Him unworthily. How could He possibly remain in such hearts where He is scourged and crowned with thorns? No one enjoys being scourged and crowned with thorns, certainly not Jesus. He tolerated it for our salvation, for love of us. He deserves to be rendered appreciation, gratitude not continuous scourging and crowning with thorns with our sinfulness, disgracing Him with our fashion. I was left with no other option than to remind the sisters, politely of course, their out-fit showed no respect for Jesus. To my utter surprise, I was made to understand it was none of my business how they dressed. Thereafter, I was thrown aghast by the reaction of their mother who would have shown understanding, but then I noticed her own clothing was not better. It then dawned on me the reason she supported them and cautioned me. Unfortunately their father who appeared somewhat to have shared my opinion seemed powerless over the attitude of his family and busied himself with cigarette smoking. How I pitied them. Naturally, no pious mother would wear such clothes on the streets, much less at Mass nor would such have dared allow her teenage daughters attend Holy Mass in such explosive fashion to dare approach the Lord in that state under her very nose. Remember St. Paul's advice, though we be in the world we should not be in conformity with the world. Bearing on mind how deeply Jesus distastes such fashion, He is the one being humiliated in the exposure of the body in sexy outfits, for the love of our Blessed Lord such fashions should be a taboo to all God's children.

The exposure of the body in sexy-outfits portray moral decay. Most sexual crimes of today are instigated by the exhibition of oneself in the name of fashion, in the attempt to attract the opposite sex. How could someone, a Catholic Christian, who is aware of the Real Presence of our Lord, dare approach Him in such disgraceful fashion in His Eucharistic presence! Has He not been humiliated enough during His passion? Why give Him the impression you support those who stripped Him and disgraced Him before the sea of people? Don't forget He is your Creator, your Destiny, above all your Heavenly Father who deserves your love and respect. It is love of us, His Children, that reduced Him to such a state, love for Humanity. To keep His Promise not to leave us as orphans He remains among us in the Host for the sanctification of our souls to enable us partake in His Divine Life eternally in Him with Him and for Him in Heaven. To take His humility for granted spells trouble, a bitter consequence. He is the Almighty God, Creator of Heaven and Earth, of all things seen and unseen, Author and giver of life. "Whoever has seen me has seen the Father" "The Father is in me and I am in the Father" Therefore, respect your God, approach Him in awe. Love Him and enjoy His fatherly love. At moment Jesus is asking you to return His love for you like a beggar, do not take His Humility for weakness. It would be wrong to wait until He comes in His glory as a righteous Judge or until you expire to face His judgement. He loves you. Everyone who loves life should keep the focus on Heaven. Heaven is worth looking forward to don't miss it! Oh, how disappointed most souls would be on seeing the Lord face to face, on seeing His Beauty, when it would be too late for them for a change. What a pity for the soul who lands in hell on his own will!

Little souls though we be, each in his uniqueness, in the enclosure of his body, with desires, ambitions, struggling for gratification of some kind, with expectations of educational, political and economic achievements for self-exaltation, according to capability in this transitory world. A permanent struggle of the soul, in his human body, which in most cases ends up in despair, disillusionment, perhaps in self destruction, due to the inability to cope with the pace of social standards. A struggle that portrays the continuous search of the soul for happiness and satisfaction in a world of moral decay, in a world of materialism, oblivious of his identity which is the key to the mystery of his existence. If only the soul would realize he is a created being, seeks his Creator who is God, finds Him in His Son Jesus Christ, embraces Him, thereby establishing a personal relationship with Him, then he will realize what he has been searching for, true happiness and tranquility and not the otherwise temporal pleasure under the camouflage of ambition for self-exaltation that leads to inevitable destruction. The surrender to Divine Love, in total giving of self to Jesus Christ, with focus on Heaven, is an assurance of an unimaginable tranquility, equilibrium and delight, a slight taste of the everlasting pleasure, the overwhelming happiness, Eternal Joy which is the fruitful reward for the soul, eternally, through grace from the Most Merciful Father.

However, having informed a priest about the above mentioned incident, in the confessional, he made me understand he would not want any one in his parish to go about correcting people on their out-fit. As I have lent my tongue to Jesus I did not agree with him seeing Jesus has no one to speak for Him but me, as a Catholic Christian. I felt it my place to represent His interest, as long as He keeps me in this Exile. Having completed His Redemptive mission and gone back to the Father, His interest must be protected, the wealth of our Catholic Faith shared with everyone. However, although I was not of the same opinion with the priest, I heard him out in silence knowing fully well Jesus will instruct me on how to carry on for the future. Nevertheless, the priest had my sympathy and understanding knowing him as a passionate priest, he was merely afraid of losing members of his congregation. Nonetheless, he tends to have forgotten, Jesus is able to make stones worship Him if He had need to do so, besides, all that the Father has given Him no-one would be able to take from Him. There is the need to caution those who expose themselves at Mass, exposing oneself is humiliating Jesus, if His bitter passion is called to mind, the scourging, the mockery and the tenth station of the cross when He was striped.

To this effect, before down, on 11.04.2013, just before waking up, I was blessed with a very beautiful dream. A display of the Supernatural, high up in the sky. Such a breath-taking beauty of military gallantry my eyes have ever set on that spoke of the Power and Majesty of the Almighty God. A gallant display of men in beautiful colorful array of mediaeval military, trooping the color in the sky. First of all, two appeared, each carrying a banner and a cross trooping the color in a bright clear sky. The breath-taking beauty of it all, its majestic captivating allure brought me kneeling down in awe, overwhelmed with admiration. All of a sudden more appeared each with a banner and a cross forming a circle as they trooped the color. It was extremely fantastic, indeed a most beautiful sight to behold. Gradually, one of them began descending down to earth as a crowd gathered to witness the spectacle. Suddenly, someone excitedly exclaimed "It's Francis of Assisi!" St. Francis of Assisi, in his life time, I understand, as a young troubadour, dreamt of a beautiful military career that would bring him honor, fame and wealth. With this on mind, as it was, he misinterpreted what was revealed to him in a dream, by Jesus Christ, concerning a vast and splendid palace with shining weapons and amours of the military which he was told was meant for him and his knights. However, he was made to realize his principality was to be of another order. Having faithfully served the Lord Jesus Christ, his Divine Master, forfeiting everything for His Love, he now enjoys His Glory, achieving his heart's desire in such a manner as he never would have dreamt of in all his earthly life, in the Supernatural, in the Divine Military of the Heavenly Kingdom of the Eternal Father. He now has his knights, his fame and wealth, his treasure in Heaven, what a grandeur!

The wonderful heavenly performance in the sky got the crowd mesmerized, everyone in utter fascination of the marvelous Supernatural Beauty high above in the sky. Suddenly, someone excitedly pointed to a girl who she referred to as the girl-friend of Francis of Assisi whom I presumed to be St. Clair of Assisi being the only girl-friend he had while on earth. Once again, just as in reality with reference to the case of the sisters wearing indecent clothes at Mass, who slighted me at my good intention in pointing out to them the mistake of wearing such clothes as it hurts Jesus, there was someone smoking in this dream close to me. Somehow, I felt inclined to warn this person against smoking due to its dangerous effect to health and was slighted, it was again not my business. Having been slighted, I felt the urge to inform the girl next to me about the ingratitude of the man but instead of the expected consolation from her she reported me to St. Clair giving a wrong version of the situation, without allowing St. Clair to hear me on the matter. She talked all alone to my dismay. Somehow, having the urge St. Clair should at least know the truth, without permission, I voiced out what the issue at steak really was. Thereafter, St. Clair gave me right. It was not wrong to have pointed out the danger of smoking to whoever it was and I felt consoled. Waking up from that beautiful dream my heart was filled with joy for this Divine revelation in support of this minute effort of mine for the love of Jesus. It is a natural inclination of mine to warn smokers, for the love of Jesus, if peradventure, by His Grace, I might be able to help someone save his life and prevent him from offending in the ten commandment "Thou shalt not kill." Smoking shortens life, no one has a right to tamper with someone's life, not even his own, life belongs to God. We do not own ourselves, God owns us. To shorten one's life with smoking is an act of suicide, knowing fully well it is harmful to health, therefore an offense to God. Such habits should be dealt away with. A frequent reception of the Sacrament of Reconciliation is advisable, with an honest desire to get rid of it for the love of Jesus. If one stumbles in the course of it, unintentionally, one should always repentantly seek Jesus in the confessional. All He wants is your trust in His Divine Mercy. Our Catholic Faith is very rich and fulfilling if only we learn to appreciate it. Jesus is always ready to help us.

Having enjoyed the company of St. Francis and St. Clair for a while, when they wanted to depart, I had the urge to go with them, but St Francis, at once, discovered there was no fuel in his Rover, which restrained me from entering into the car to sit down, but St. Clair entered and sat down. On waking up from this beautiful dream I realized the reason St. Francis referred to the lack of fuel was to prevent me from following them because it was not time for me to join them in Heaven. This beautiful dream, was a consolation, a confirmation, to me, of the necessity, as a Catholic Christian, to be a witness for Christ by practicing my Catholic Faith. I should not close my eyes to things that hurt Jesus. The world needs God, but she is blinded by the foolishness of her wisdom, therefore, it is the duty of every Catholic Christian to bring Jesus to every none Catholic, to the world, for Jesus to heal them. Gently pointing out error cannot be wrong rather it is a help to a soul for his salvation. It didn't matter if one is slighted in the course of it, all it takes is to bear it for the love of Jesus. If one kept one's focus on the cross any insult would be accepted, as Love from our Good Lord in His loving attempt to teach us the Virtue of Humility. This dream clearly points out Jesus is displeased when He is approached without reverence in the Blessed Sacrament. To approach Him improperly dressed hurts His Most Sacred Heart. His Majesty is so great, the all Powerful, Holy and Immortal God, Author and Giver of Life, Lord of Heaven and Earth should be approached with respect, in awe and in deepest humility. It is the Holy Trinity, the Highest God in the Sacrament of His Love. It is wise to reverence His Divine Presence. Moreover, the Divine Presence of the Holy Trinity fills the Holy Sanctuary, the Tabernacle, which calls for the approach with awe, realizing at the same time the need to be silent in the Church which is a House of prayer, not a market place for chatting, but for contemplation in preparation for the celebration of the Mass and for the reception of our Lord Jesus Christ in the Holy Eucharist, the Sacrament of His Love.

The souls radiate the Glory of God, beautiful little souls in godly forms they are, as they proceed from God, possessing His nature, God's little Children created by Him out of love, for love and infinitely loved by Him, but trapped, so to say, in their humanity due to sin originated in the fall of Adam and Eve. To restore to the souls their original beauty and heritage God took flesh to destroy death forever, the wage of sin. God is Love and Love is Beauty, Love is Eternal, therefore, souls being from God are Love, Beauty and Eternal. God has delight in souls, they are His Children. If a mother would forget her child, God would not, being the best Father. His love for souls, His children, emerged into a motherly love. This infinite love of God for souls instigated His incarnation, in the second person of the Trinity, being the only possible way. A created being could not atone for sin therefore, the Word took Flesh for His Love for souls, to free them from Satan, the cause of the fall of man. To save them from death, which is the wage of sin, reconcile them with God the Father, restore life to them, and open for them the gate of Heaven for Eternal life with Him, in Him and for Him. God is the Origin, Destiny and Destination of every soul made for Heaven. The awareness of this should instigate every soul to seek God's Grace to find himself in God and love Him Who is the Father of all souls in order to realize his true identity, Love. It is wisely said that like terms beget like terms, therefore, God being Beauty begets beautiful souls and as such there is no ugly soul. It does not matter if someone is physically disabled or not, he is not ugly though the flesh may appear to be, but what makes a soul ugly, however, is sin. When a soul rejects the salvation won for souls by Jesus Christ that soul remains, in the darkness and ugliness of sin, dirty and ugly on his own free-will. That soul consequently loses every relationship with God and ends up in eternal damnation with his own free-will.

Nothing ugly and dirty has a share in God who is Beautiful, Holy, Pure and Divine. God Who is Love wants to lavish man with love. Every soul who loves God will realize his beauty when he beholds the dazzling Beauty of God on his departure from this exile back to God his Father. He would be dumbfounded with God's Beauty which he himself will radiate. But the soul who, of his own choice, remained in the ugliness of sin by rejecting God's Love, the salvation won for humanity by His Beloved Son Jesus, would be faced with the bitter truth of perdition, the fate which he chose for himself. He would be deprived of the Beauty of God forever. He would spend eternity in hell eternally. God so loves humanity He would not tamper with his free-will. Heaven is a wonderful place of joy eternal. The beauty of Heaven cannot be described with words but one can allow imagination play her role. If humanity is so fascinated with the magnificent creation of this world, with her natural beauty, with all the natural sceneries, the majestic mountains and prominent hills, the seas and the vast oceans with their inhabitants, the green vegetation's, the forests home of beautiful assortments of wild life, the firmament and so much more, that depicts the hand-writing of a Most Wonderful Creator, a Loving Father Who has the comfort and happiness of His Children at Heart, how fascinated would we be when we behold the breath-taking Beauty of Heaven the abode of His Supreme Majesty, the Eternal Father, God of Creation, the Almighty God to whom all that is belongs. By Him there is no lack, no sorrow, sickness nor death but joy eternal, every one forever young, enjoying the Father's Love. What a life to look forward to with all anticipation and excitement, the Beatific Vision, the Father's Love for His Children, little souls, to share in His Divine Life of Glory and Beauty.

CHAPTER VII

THE EUCHARIST

The beauty of life is love, without love life is meaningless. Every one searches and reaches out for love. But how can one know one is loved without the proof of love? Of course, there are different types of love, but the love above all love is the love of self-sacrifice, agape, self-giving, pure innocent love as described in St. Paul's first epistle to the Corinthians "Love is patient and kind; love is not jealous or boastful; It is not arrogant or rude. Love does not insist on its own way; It is not irritable or resentful; it does not rejoice at wrong, but rejoices in the right. Love bears all things, believes all things, hopes all things, endures all things. Love never ends...." This describes the nature of God Who is love. It well explains His humility and the sacrifice of Jesus Christ Who emptied Himself for love of us, for humanity. Despite the human weakness, the graveness of sin which He hates like the pest, He forgives, regardless of how often we fail Him, if our repentance is genuine, not willful sin, whereby His Divine Mercy is taken for granted. That notwithstanding the sinner is still loved because God is Love. He will never cease from loving. God, in His infinite Mercy left humanity with living proofs of His Divine love. God has been Faithful in every way to man, but man leaves Him in agony constantly hurting Him.

To prove His love for humanity God took Flesh and became sin to reconcile man to Himself. He lived the humblest of life of poverty. "Foxes have holes, but the son of man has nowhere to lay his head" What a lesson for those in love with pomp and riches of this world that will be destroyed by fire, the head of states drunk with power at the expense of their subjects, the Kings and queens, who parade with nose held up in the air hanging on palaces and wealth that are of no benefit to them when this earthly life expires, to learn. The owner of wealth, His Supreme Majesty, has nowhere to lay His head. That His Divine Majesty to whom we all owe our existence, from whom all knowledge and wisdom come, Author and Giver of life, Omniscience, Omnipotent, Lord of Heaven and Earth, for His love of us, had nowhere to lay His Head in His own Land, is most admirable and praiseworthy. This leaves one wondering at the great interest humanity has in materialism, the alacrity and greed with which wealth is pursued in this sinful and transient world. Of what value is it after all in accumulating wealth, when the owner of it, in His earthly life, rejected it. The problem, however, is not in the wealth itself, but how it is spent. If wealth is honestly earned and shared to the benefit of the less favored, giving glory to God the Giver of all that is good, it would in turn be a blessing, otherwise, it becomes a burden to the soul that possesses it, as it becomes his master. Every good position in the public life is a gift from God for the common good, to be spent to His Glory therefore, the poor should not be neglected. What we are and what we achieve are all out of His Goodness. By bearing this on mind, keeping His precepts, we abide in His Love. After all, the focus on Heaven with strong determination, not minding the cost, is holy wisdom. "There is great gain in godliness with contentment" For those who love God no sacrifice is too much. With true love for God the burden becomes light.

It is amazing the enthusiasm with which the media announced the birth of the prince, son of Duke and Duchess of Cambridge, William and Kate, over their first baby. Observing the thrill the news of this royal birth gave to the world, the military artillery gun salute of twenty-one shots, the pride of the British people as a nation, the congratulatory messages sent from heads of states of several countries and royalties, one cannot help, in retrospect, to see the contrast between this royal birth and the Supreme Royal Birth of the Supreme Royal Baby, our Lord Jesus Christ, the Divine Child, by whom all things were made, visible and invisible, the Incarnate Son of the Most High God, Who was born in a stable, laid in a manger and wrapped in a swaddling cloth. The congratulatory message to His poor parents was a threat to His Divine life which consequently led to the death of numerous innocent children under the age of two. Yes, the birth of the prince, third in line to the British throne, is of course, a thing of joy, but is it justified to find in the congratulatory messages no expression of gratitude to the Giver of such a wonder that sent almost the whole world into ecstasy. Would the status of the parents, grandparents and also the great grandparents of the poor prince diminish if any of them, if not all, expressed before the media their gratitude to the good God who endowed them with a bouncing baby prince. One should not forget in plenty, the parable of the rich man who was so obsessed in his worldly goods and praised himself for having enough for a life time, so much so he would not have to work again. But when his soul was demanded of him he had no time any more to eat and enjoy that which he so much treasured, his worldly goods. All his much treasured goods were useless to him then. The Lord Jesus aimed at imparting to humanity the need for gratitude, to realize all we are, all we have achieved, are all from God the Father of humanity. Therefore, in everything, small or big an expression of gratitude to the Almighty Father, who, in His infinite goodness endows humanity with such beautiful gifts in life would not be wrong. Moreover, whether we eat or drink, happy or sad, in every condition we should give thanks to God whose every act is love, even if we do not understand, we should simply trust in Him. Sometime, somehow He will make it plain. Without God's infinite Love and Mercy humanity would cease to exist. Of what use is it then to neglect God, the Giver of life, for worldly riches and pomp, to end up in perdition, where there is no riches and pomp? God alone is security, peace and tranquility here below and Eternal Joy in Heaven. God alone matters, nothing else!

The world grasps at nothing, reaches out to emptiness, what the world thinks to be, is not. Therefore, that which seems to be and is not should be treated with mindfulness as its ultimate fate is transient. Nevertheless, the Divine child, Jesus, despite all obstacles, grew in age wisdom and grace. At the age of thirty He began His ministry, the proclamation of the Kingdom of God for a period of three years in which He performed many miracles. Jesus Christ, the incarnate Word of God, gave to humanity a clear revelation of God in Himself. God alone is the only source of credibility to Himself, therefore Jesus Christ is God when He says He is. He clearly stressed this fact when He said "Whoever sees me has seen the Father. The Father and I are one" "The Father is in me and I am in the Father" "When you have lifted up the Son of Man then you will know that I am He" He taught and spoke with authority unlike any one before Him and after Him. Despite His authoritative manner of speech, the performance of miracles, and His command of nature that proved His Divinity He was met with antagonism from the Pharisees and Sadducees, the scribes who, out of envy, sought to take His life. Having accused Him of making Himself, being a man, equal to God, they finally succeeded in making Pilate, a gentile, condemn Him to death, though he found no fault in Him, for making Himself King of the Jews. This Jesus, who came that the world may have life and have it more abundantly, full of compassion for humanity surrendered, without compulsion, Himself to the verdict of the Roman procurator, Pontius Pilate, death by crucifixion, taking upon Himself the wages of sin for humanity. Long before His Incarnation was due He made it known, through many prophets, including king David in his psalms, about the coming of the messiah and all he had to suffer. These prophesies about His suffering were consequently, to the last detail, fulfilled in Him. Jesus, the Messiah, Son of the living God, the Word made Flesh dwelt among us, but the world did not recognize Him. He was tortured beyond recognition. The depth of the pain He bore on His Blessed Body, all He suffered, physically and mentally are not all known, some are experienced by those fortunate souls He grants the grace to share with Him His suffering, each according to the measure of His grace. His suffering on the whole was beyond human endurance.

The forces of darkness, Satan and his subordinates, intended to kill Him to own the world they neither created nor does it belong to them. Little did they know that Love cannot be killed. Love is Life. Love never dies. Love is beautiful and sweet. God is Love. Wickedness is ugly. It is death, therefore, Satan is wickedness, ugly and death. Jesus, the most loving Savior, endured to the end with the power of the Love in His Most Sacred Heart, won the battle with His victorious Cross, opened the Gate of Heaven, and secured life for humanity with His glorious Resurrection, the triumph against the power of darkness by conquering death. Jesus emptied Himself for our redemption, what remains is individual acceptance of it by personal effort through His grace and trust in Him. In order to accomplish this Jesus left us with the Sacraments to be administered to the Faithful by the Church, His Mystical Body, the One, Holy, Catholic and Apostolic Church with St. Peter, the Pope as His Vicar.

This beautiful, wonderful, sweet Love of Jesus for humanity, instigated Him to institute the Sacrament of the Eucharist the evening before His passion. He offered Himself as food under the appearances of bread and wine, a sacramental expression of the Easter Mystery. In so doing He testified His Love for humanity for whose Salvation He would offer Himself in Sacrifice. The Eucharist is Jesus Himself and not a symbol as the protestant and evangelist churches presume when they receive communion. Jesus is truly Man and truly God, whatever He says is. When He broke the bread and gave to His apostles as His Body and the wine as His Blood, He was actually holding His Body and Blood in His own Divine Hands which He gave to His apostles to eat and drink and to celebrate as often as possible in memory of Him. He conferred to them the authority to be Him, His priests, to offer Him to the members of His Mystical Body, the Church. One cannot help but point out the danger in not receiving Jesus in the Eucharist. As Jesus strictly pointed out in Jn 6 vs. 51-53 that His Flesh is food indeed therefore, to have life one must eat Him and drink His Blood. That the Church should remain one is an indelible desire of Jesus Christ, hence the Church is His Mystical Body, this fact emphasizes the essentiality to partake in the Holy Eucharist, the Supper of the Lamb by which He gradually transforms us so as to share in His Divine Life. This irrevocable truth, therefore calls for an urgent return of none Catholics to the One, Holy, Catholic and Apostolic Church founded by Jesus on Peter in order to be grafted into the Vine, so as to keep His commandment, partake in the supper of the Lamb and abide in His love. This way the members of His Mystical Body would be back to normal, everyone partaking in the life giving Eucharist, His Body, Blood, Soul and Divinity and be nourished to share in His Divine Life. Unfortunately no amount of argument can change the truth. Jesus is the Truth. He is the Way the Truth and the Life. He gave His all for His Church, for humanity. It cost Him His most precious Blood to found His Church. His Arms are wide open for all who hear His voice and hearken to it. "Abide in My Love" "Love one another as I have loved you" Be ye one as I and my Father are one" If you love me keep my commandment". The Eucharist is the source and summit of the Catholic Faith to be received only by the Faithful who believe in the real Presence of Jesus Christ. The Holy Eucharist is Jesus Christ, Body, Blood, Soul and Divinity.

It is not advisable for any priest to encourage protestants, none Catholics to receive the Holy Eucharist even if they believe in the real Presence, as some priests in Germany do aiming at ecumenism. If a none Catholic believes in the real Presence of our Lord, then what stops him from becoming Catholic to receive the Lord worthily. Jesus Himself condemns receiving Him unworthily and so does Saint Paul, as he clearly states in his epistle. Any priest who encourages this does not favor himself nor the recipient who eats unworthily against the Holy Will of God causing Jesus to be tied up and beaten in the hearts of those who receive Him unworthily. Jesus was scourged enough during His passion, let no one scourge Him any more by receiving Him unworthily. To receive His Supreme Majesty, such a highly prominent Visitor one should be descent enough to tidy up his home to keep such a Visitor comfortable to enable Him remain with him, after all He provided the means to do so at His Mercy Seat in the confessional, the Sacrament of Reconciliation. One must not forget it is judgement to eat the Lord Jesus Christ unworthily. It is not the place of any one to change the ordinances of God at will. It is not about us but about God.

How sad some priests indulge in sin, living adulterous life, having illegal children without bothering about the feeling of their Divine Master, while some engage themselves with worldly possessions even at the risk of perdition. How could such priests dare keep our Good Lord willfully in agony! Do they think they would eat their cake and have it merely because Jesus is a Merciful God? Do they ever think they would someday give an account of their life to God? or do they think being simply a priest is a ticket to Heaven, it didn't matter whatever conduct they have? Such priests should cease from staining the image of priests. There are a good number of passionate loyal priests who realize their reward is in Heaven. These priests are a consolation to Jesus. One cannot serve God and Mammon, Jesus made this clear. Nevertheless, it does not matter if the priest is sinful or not, Jesus will see to that when the time is ripe, what matters now is that the Faithful need Him, He loves them and desires to nourish their souls with His Body and Blood so as to transform them to enable them be with Him where He is and partake in the Beatific Vision, in His Glory, eternally in Heaven. Nevertheless, these priests who practice the opposite of what they preach should cease from deceiving themselves, return penitently to their Divine Master and cease from sin before the darkness falls.

Unfortunately, there are, today, a good number of priests who have left their priestly habits to decay in their wardrobes, who run about in ordinary clothes looking just like the guy next door. Such priests expose themselves to temptation, to Satan the crafty enemy, who is insatiably seeking the downfall of priests. Jesus did not come to change the law but to fulfil it therefore, if we believe that God always is, then believe also it is not His desire His priests should run about in plain clothes. After all, God took pains to describe to Moses the priestly vestments of Aaron and his sons. Do not forget you serve a righteous God. His desire for His priests to appear different from the rest has not changed because God is.

The Eucharist is Holy. It is the Holy Trinity. It is Jesus, Body, Blood, Soul and Divinity. Where Jesus is, the Father and the Holy Spirit also are therefore, the Holy Eucharist is to be received with respect, in awe and in humility. In the awareness of the Godhead in the Holy Eucharist, bearing on mind man's unworthiness, it is most advisable to receive the Holy Eucharist in the mouth. Jesus appreciates and desires to be received in the mouth. It infuses awesomeness in the individual and calls for respect for the Most Supreme Majesty, the Almighty God. The reception of the Holy Eucharist in the hand makes Him become too common, tarnishing with time, the feeling of awe, especially among children and the youth. God's humility should not be taken for granted. At least, all the faithful should receive the infinite Love His Most Sacred Heart has to offer in gratitude. A complete misunderstanding of the Vatican II led to the laxity in the reverence of God which consequently, gave rise to the scarcity of priests and lack of vocation for consecrated lives, especially in Europe. As a result, in some countries like Germany, women now distribute the Holy Eucharist, a task meant for priests and deacons alone. Consequent to lack of priests, whose place it is to bring the Lord to sick ones in their homes, relatives now take Him to them instead. This practice is being misused by some of the faithful who seize the opportunity of bringing Holy Communion to sick relations to relations who do not attend mass any more, have not been for years in the confessional and are not sick. Such a practice is sacrilege. One only needs to bring a pix, place it on the offertory table, the priest then puts the consecrated Host in it. Some priests no longer emphasize the danger in receiving the Lord unworthily. This is a serious matter, the faithful should be constantly reminded and warned of sacrilege. Moreover, every faithful should be aware of hell and Heaven so as not to precipitate into the danger of taking the Lord's Mercy for granted and lose their soul. At least every Catholic Christian should be in the position to practice the basics of our Catholic Faith genuinely. There is, however, a woman, in my parish, praying for her son to begin to attend Mass again so, for this purpose she takes our Lord, in a pix, regularly home to him in the hope our Lord would convert him. Unfortunately the priest gives our Lord to her, each time, without any inquiries about the improvement of the health of whoever it is she takes our good Lord to. This is absurd! Jesus strictly warned against receiving Him unworthily. It is not enough to receive Him, one must be in a state of grace. It is still the same Lord Jesus Christ before the Vatican II. The Lord does not change, He is the same forever. His Ordinances are to be respected and honored.

Actually, the son of the above mentioned woman in my parish used to come to the church on Saturdays only to bring flower and light candle for prayer before the blessed Virgin Mary without staying for mass. Having observed him several times I felt compelled to inform him about the need to stay for mass. He promised he would but never did. Nevertheless, on one Saturday I made inquiries to find out from him when his last confession was, he could not remember as it was a long decade, but informed me his mother usually brings him the Holy Communion at home. I was shocked and felt pity for the sacrilege he induces his mother to commit. However, his mother informed me later he has not been to confession for the past ten years. On the long run, he stopped bringing flowers on Saturdays. However, his mother informed me he has lost interest completely in the Church yet she continued to take Holy Communion to him. Poor Jesus, how He must feel seeing all the sacrilege, profanations, and indifference to His Person, in His Humility for the love of humanity. Why should we allow our good Lord to keep weeping. However, with the help of the Lord, I was able to convince her to make a thorough confession, to stop giving the priest the impression her son is sick, in order to obtain mercy from the Lord and be free from the sin of sacrilege so as to have peace. Moreover, I advised she should have patience with the Lord and keep praying. Surprisingly, this advice was taken which did her good as she felt better. The tension in her eased off. The Lord who loves so much, so infinitely, does not deserve the treatment He is oftentimes given. It is most important for parents to instruct their children on the Catholic Faith from their tender age, while they themselves practice it, as example for their children, to enable them grow up rooted in their catholic faith, loving Jesus from the heart with respect and awe. Have pity on the Most Sacred Heart of Jesus. Nevertheless, it would not be wrong if priests from time to time remind the Laity, in their Homilies, the need to receive Jesus worthily in the Sacrament of His Love, making known to them what Sacrilege is, the need for penance, sacrifice, from time to time and to make sincere efforts for a holy life.

The Church is a Body, an organism, She is alive and She has a Soul. The Holy Spirit is the Soul of the Church. As God is one so also is the Church one, although she has many members. The Faith which we practice is one and alive. Jesus Christ shed His Most Precious Blood to found His Church. Remember the persistent repetition of Jesus about the need to eat His Flesh and drink His Blood without bothering if He lost all His disciples because He was revealing an irreversible truth in Jn.6 vs 51 – 68. "I am the living bread which came down from heaven; if any man eats of this bread, he will live forever; and the bread which I shall give for the life of the world is my flesh." Therefore, receive Him worthily, preferably in the mouth, with respect and awe. Give reverence to the Most Holy Trinity!

The Jews disputed among themselves, saying, "How can this man give us his flesh to eat?" Then Jesus said to them Truly, truly, I say to you, unless you eat the flesh of the Son of man and drink his blood, you have no life in you; he who eats my flesh and drinks my blood has eternal life, and I will raise him up at the last day. For my flesh is food indeed, and my blood is drink indeed. He who eats my flesh and drinks my blood abides in me, and I in him. As the living Father sent me, and I live because of the Father, so he who eats me will live because of me. This is the bread which came down from heaven, not such as the fathers ate and died; he who eats this bread will live forever" This he said in the synagogue, as he taught at Capernaum. Many of his disciples, when they heard of it, said, "This is a hard saying; who can listen to it?" But Jesus, knowing in himself that his disciples murmured at it, said to them, "Do you take offense at this? Then what if you were to see the son of man ascending where he was before? It is the spirit that gives life, the flesh is of no avail; the words that I have spoken to you are spirit and life. But there are some of you that do not believe."

For Jesus knew from the first who those were that did not believe, and who it was that would betray him. And he said, "This is why I told you that no one can come to me unless it is granted him by the Father." After this many of his disciples drew back and no longer went about with him. Jesus said to the twelve, "Will you also go away?" Simon Peter, the spokesman of the apostles, as the future Pope, answered, "Lord, to whom shall we go? You have the words of eternal life; and we have believed, and have come to know, that you are the Holy One of God"

Jesus spoke in His authority as the Most Supreme Majesty and whatever He says is. Furthermore, humanity, having been destined by God the Father to spend Eternity with Him eternally in Heaven, have the need to be transformed into the nature of God which is Love. Therefore, in order to accomplish this the sinful nature of man must be consumed in God's Love by the assimilation of Jesus Christ Himself, Body, Blood, Soul and Divinity in the Most Holy Sacrament, the Holy Eucharist. This way we become one with the Holy Trinity, Father, Son and the Holy Spirit in Jesus Christ. Therefore, through Jesus Christ we become intimate with the Holy Trinity Who makes His abode in our souls. Then we can have a personal relationship with our God in Jesus Christ. The Eucharist is thanksgiving, the Gift of God of Himself to humanity. This beautiful Gift of God of Himself in the Eucharist should instigate every Christian to hunger for the Lord, to share in the supper of the Lamb, in the Holy Eucharist, the source and summit of the Christian Faith. This is the Sacred Desire of the Most Sacred Heart of Jesus Christ. If all Christian denominations, with a sincere desire to abide in the Love of Jesus Christ, the keeping of His commandments, would retrace their steps back to their roots, the One Holy, Catholic and Apostolic Church founded by Jesus Christ Himself upon Peter, our good Lord would cease from being in Agony. If there be a sincere desire to serve God, not selfish aims, then humility, which is the perfect Virtue of the Highest God, of Jesus Christ whom we claim to serve, would be priority, then the one good thing that would delight His Most Sacred Heart, a return Home to His Holy Church, to His Body, would take place, for all to share in His Body and Blood, the Bread of Life for Eternal Life with Him in Heaven.

Nevertheless, I cannot help but wonder at the sincerity of the protestant churches, the evangelist churches, and the rest of them for ecumenism. Are they actually seeking a return to the true Faith or are they just simply making headlines in the media with talks about ecumenism. One should not forget that God is not a respecter of persons. He should not be taken for granted. "If we say we have fellowship with him while we walk in darkness, we lie and do not live according to the truth" 1st Jn 1 vs 6. How could a pastor of the evangelist church in Germany proudly announce to the media He got homosexuals married in his church. Why should one allow himself to be an instrument of Satan, trying the patience of the Best and Most Merciful God. Does common sense not make him realize he should be ashamed to announce proudly the abominations he committed? Marriage is a sacrament instituted by Jesus Christ Himself "Therefore, shall a man leave his father and mother, and shall cleave unto his wife: and they shall be one flesh" Gen.2 vs 24. They are no more two but one. Marriage is for procreation between a man and a woman and not between same sex. It was indeed very heart-rending hearing this ugly news in the media. If I felt this way, how would the Most Sacred Heart of Jesus feel? One should not forget this world is transitory, the life in this world has its end and afterwards one has to face this God Who has done so much for humanity, Who is willing to share His Divine Life with humanity eternally in Eternity. A God of Love Who has suffered so much for humanity, yet do not forget He is a Righteous Judge. It is His Divine Will for every soul to be saved, but turning the back to His Love, the soul must then face His judgement. To reject God is to reject life on one's own free-will. This evangelist pastor is not the only pastor who has committed this abomination but be ye warned, you are trading on dangerous ground. Due to same sex relationships nations like Gomorrah and Sodom have been stamped out of the surface of the earth. It is still the same God, He does not change. God did not create any one with same sex inclinations such is caused from dirty minds and the inability to put flesh under subjection. This abominations from hell can be overcome if one sought assistance from God who is more than willing to assist if one made one self docile to receive His sanctifying Grace.

Presenting obstacles to a common objective does not certify the sincerity of the intentions of those from whom the obstacles come. If ecumenism is of great importance to protestant churches why do they subject themselves to creating conditions against the precepts of God? Conditions which present barriers to the unity of the Body of Christ, the Church. The separation from the Holy See, being insubordinate to the Pope was an offence to our Lord. It tore the Body of the Lord to pieces. Now ecumenism strives to reunite Christendom. But it is sad how those concerned go about it. The introduction of women priests, acceptance of same-sex relationships, ordination of homosexual and women bishops are factors that speak against ecumenism, practiced by protestant churches. Our God is a Holy God and those who serve Him must serve Him in truth and in holiness. Has the Vatican not been generous enough to have extended a brotherly hand to the Anglican

Church when Pope Benedict XVI emeritus created room for her to come back to her roots? The Archbishop of Canterbury is not ignorant of the Truth of God. Therefore, acting against God's Law to please man rather than God by supporting the above mentioned evil is an offence to His Divine Majesty to which he must give an account before His Heavenly Throne. Bishops are the line of Apostles therefore, men only are to be ordained Bishops and not women. Jesus did not select women Apostles but men and ordained them Priests. If He had need for women Apostles and women Priests He would have seen to it. The Almighty God must be obeyed and served according to His Holy Will. God alone matters, no one else and nothing else.

It is most advisable for the leaders of all Churches who have torn themselves away from the Mystical Body of Christ, from His One Holy, Catholic and Apostolic Church which He founded with a bitter price, the shading of His Most Precious Blood, to accept now His Divine Mercy and come back Home while the sun shines. The Mercy of God rules His judgement. He will continue to show Mercy until the end of the world. It all depends on you to accept His Divine Mercy or reject it. Being away from His Church is being away from the Family of God. How could you be so adamant while Jesus is tenderly calling you to come home so you can inherit the Kingdom of your Heavenly Father prepared for you from the beginning of the world? You cannot give the Almighty God pretended devotion. You must submit yourselves totally to His Holy Will in love, in complete obedience. The Greek orthodox Church for instance, is in possession of the complete knowledge of the truth. Andrew must reunite with Peter for this is God's Holy Will. You are aware Jesus chose Peter as His Vicar, therefore, remember His prayer for unity in John 17, swallow your pride, be humble as your Divine Master and Savior is humble, reunite yourself to Rome, be subordinate to the Pope according to the Holy Will of our Lord Jesus Christ. One cannot serve God as one chooses but as God wants to be served. Anything short of this is selfishness, arrogance, greed, unfaithfulness, and disobedience to the Almighty God.

Ezekiel 33 vs 8 – 9 says "If I say to the wicked, O wicked man, you shall surely die, and you do not speak to warn the wicked to turn from his way, that wicked man shall die in his iniquity, but his blood I will require at your hand. But if you warn the wicked to turn from his way, and he does not turn from his way; he shall die in his iniquity, but you will have saved your life." There is no need for sweet-talking but to hit the nail on the head. It is always advisable to bear on mind "Not everyone who says to me, 'Lord Lord,' shall enter the kingdom of heaven, but he who does the will of my father who is in heaven. On that day many will say to me, 'Lord, Lord, did we not prophesy in your name, and cast out demons in your name, and do many mighty works in your name?' And then will I declare to them, 'I never knew you; depart from me, you evildoers."

CHAPTER VIII

SELF ESTEEM

The one thing humanity does with enthusiasm in which he derives great pleasure is in his achievements, his capabilities, his so called 'know how'. There is no age limit to this vanity, though it is much rampant among the adults. Today, in this age of female awareness that which was mostly attributed to men, the competitive drive for success and self-exaltation, is now prominent in women. The role of women, as mothers of the nations, their God-given role of taking care of the home and raising up healthy children with good morals for a better co-existence among all peoples, has been neglected in the pursuit of fame, position, profession, thereby rubbing shoulders with the masculine world.

The saying a woman is domestic, her place is in the kitchen has lost its meaning, as it seems, to most women, outdated. But little did these women realize it is a blessing in disguise. Indeed a woman's place is the kitchen. Her place is to spend her love for the family. A loving and subordinate wife is a treasure to her husband and children. "Happy is the husband of a good wife; the number of his days will be doubled. A loyal wife rejoices her husband, and he will complete his years in peace. A good wife is a great blessing; she will be granted among the blessings of the man who fears the Lord. Whether rich or poor, his heart is glad, and at all times his face is cheerful. A wife's charm delights her husband, and her skill puts fat on his bones. A silent wife is a gift of the Lord, and there is nothing so precious as a disciplined soul. A modest wife adds charm to charm, and no balance can weigh the value of a chaste soul. Like the sun rising in the heights of the Lord, so is the beauty of a good wife in her well-ordered home. Like the shining lamp on the holy lampstand, so is a beautiful face on a stately figure. Like pillars of gold on a base of silver, so are beautiful feet with a steadfast heart." Sirach 26 vs 1 – 4, 13 – 18. Should a woman crown her love for her husband and children with the love of God, making Jesus her focus and Heaven her ultimate goal, she would have won for her family a calm sea, the protection of the Supernatural, the Divine protection of the Almighty God. If only women realized their value, without rubbing shoulders with the men, the society of the world today would have been a lot healthier, paving way to a better understanding and knowledge of the Almighty God, the Author and Giver of life, Lord of Heaven and Earth. It would have ushered in Christ's glorious reign of peace and sorrow would be no more.

Nevertheless, the masculine world, express their displeasure with feminism in different ways, such as in the creation of provocative clothing to dishonor the female body under the camouflage of fashion, portraying women as objects of lust, a weapon of disrespect, an indirect cry for the golden age when women used to shine in the glory with which they are clothed by the God of creation. The ultimate provocative fashions serve as instruments to expose women as prey, to the canal inclination of the masculine world, for discarding their garment of glory to rub shoulders with the masculine world. Therefore, women became for those incapable of putting flesh under subjection, although the ability to do so has been endowed to humanity by the Almighty God, objects of lust, ushering in the sin from hell to the displeasure of the Almighty God, the Author and Giver of Life. Woman is the beauty of man to be respected, loved, and taken care of. It is a man's place to respect every woman as the weaker vessel glorifying God in her for His wonderful beautiful creation of the channel through which He sends new lives into the world as tiny sweet babies who in turn grow into maturity to fill the earth. The mystery and wonder of creation. A man is created for procreation, he has a right to marry if he cannot endure, to become one with his wife and love her as Jesus loves His Church. "Husbands, love your wives, as Christ loved the church and gave himself up for her, that he might sanctify her, having cleansed her by the washing of water with the word, that he might present the church to himself in splendor, without spot or wrinkle or any such thing, that she might be holy and without blemish. Even so husbands should love their wives as their own bodies. He who loves his wife loves himself. For no man ever hates his own flesh, but nourishes and cherishes it, as Christ does the church, because we are members of his body." Eph. 5 vs 25 – 30

Unfortunately everyone wants to demonstrate his 'know how' which consequently results to social instability, depression, irrationality among the less favored, the result of the inability to tackle the alacrity in the pursuit of these achievements and the flamboyancy of the 'know how'. This leads to social and moral decay generated by the influence of evil whereby exists a great tendency of drifting away from the loving Father of humanity, the Almighty God without whom the soul of man knows no rest. The pursuit of wealth, achievements in the political arena, sports, show business and so on, the urge to always be in the spotlights, among the so called VIPs, do not procure to man the desired end which is peace of mind and happiness. The flamboyancy of it all is merely a camouflage of the tumult of the soul that lies beneath. The world cannot give true and lasting happiness and unless man realizes his identity as the child of God, embracing and resting on Him, man would not know peace.

It is most sad humanity is so blind, unable to recognize God's beautiful Love for man which guarantees peace and tranquility, yet that notwithstanding, humanity is blessed, for God in His infinite Goodness, continues to plead with man to return to Him. The reciprocation of God's Love is the answer to the puzzles of all that bothers the human mind concerning the happenings in the world. A genuine repentance is always acceptable to God. O how blessed is man, for Jesus does not expect perfection, though He desires the aspiration to it. However, He expects a sincere rejection of sin. Should one have a setback, not willfully though, Jesus expects genuine repentance, the trust in His Divine Mercy and in His Grace. All it takes is opening up of the heart to the God who loves man with an Infinite Love.

Nevertheless, man's problem lies in his greed for self-esteem. In pursuit of self-glory man builds up a barrier between himself and God. In so doing, on his own accord, he creates a fertile soil in his soul for the enemy, Satan, to cause him to drift away from God, whereby he is fed with the notion 'there is no God'. This way he swims in darkness to the joy of Satan the father of lies, the enemy of man, an impostor, the master of self-esteem, who with craftiness leads man to perdition. The question is, is it worth it? To rob your Heavenly Father, who loves you infinitely, the joy of fatherhood, yourself the eternal joy in your Heavenly Father's kingdom, to end up in hell with Satan. Do you realize your atheism does not eradicate God's existence. Even Satan, the father of lies, knows that God exists. The disbelief of Truth does not make Truth not to be Truth. All of humanity is created by God, without God there would be no creation and God alone sustains all that He created. Humanity is alive because of God. Whatever humanity has achieved and will achieve is all because of God. Without God man is nothing and knows nothing. Therefore, whatever one achieves, glory should be given to God and not to self. If man would realize he is nothing, realize he is wretched without God, then man would be in a better position to realize God's love in himself which would ultimately awaken the urge to observe the precepts of God to please Him Who created him. This would instigate an honest desire to know God, then with perseverance God would make Himself known and man would believe and would have peace. This is a simple formula to everlasting happiness, with God the Father, eternally in Heaven.

However, achievement in itself is not wrong. After all, God endowed man with different talents having created him in His own image. God desires man to explore and enjoy His creation to His Glory. It is improper for man to make achievements his god, take the glory which belongs to God for himself showing no gratitude to God the Giver, who blessed him with his success. On watching some young man, a surfer, proudly giving account of his bravery and the fun he derives in surfing on very terrifying waves on the sea, I listened to hear him give glory to God who created the sea and such beautiful terrifying waves to enable him have such fun but unfortunately I heard nothing to that effect, only about his 'know how' and fun. Frankly speaking, my sympathy reaches out to such people who are blind in their conceit. Little did this young man realize it is God's love that sustained him. Had it not been for God's Most Merciful Love anything would have happened to him. If the waves had over powered him and he lost his life, his soul would have gone to face God's judgement. The problem is, would he have been ready to meet God, His Creator face to face? He should be grateful to God who kept him alive to work out his salvation for Heaven and not to end up in perdition. God in His Infinite Mercy grants everyone a good measure of opportunity to seek Him, find Him and reciprocate His Love. It would be foolishness to turn a deaf ear to God. It is wise to be mindful, God will not stand and knock forever, therefore open the door of your heart and let Him in while you have the opportunity. Furthermore, the master of the house does not know when the thief comes, therefore it is appropriate to be ready at all time.

Unfortunately, this young man is not the only one who has fallen prey to conceit. In the field of science and technology, for instance, where God can easily be seen in His creation, admired for His gift of Knowledge to man to discover and learn more about his environment, the human body, about the world in which he lives, share in God's creativity, to provide devices to ease the difficulties of everyday life, in medicine, to find means of averting ailments as much as possible for good health, and glorify God, but instead, man attributes his achievements to his 'know how.' He precipitates into pride, to self-esteem. Rather than give God the Glory due to Him, man swims in his own glory. Both the scientist, the technician, the physician operate on borrowed 'know how' from the Creator, working from what God has already created, on knowledge granted at the Mercy of the Creator. Some athlete jumps from a very high skyscraper, he rejoices at his 'know how', ungrateful to the God who spared him from being food for the vulture, providing him the opportunity to reciprocate God's love for him in order to be with God, his Father, in Heaven. Pride is an attribute of the fallen nature of man inherited from the first parents, Adam and Eve, through sin. God in His infinite Mercy, at the fullness of time, sent His only begotten Son, by His Life death and resurrection, won salvation for humanity. Jesus, with His earthly Life, paved way for man to emulate Him, who being rich became poor to make us rich in Heaven. Man has the potentials to leave a life in God's Love by keeping His commandments. Jesus Christ, the Word Incarnate, who is both God and Man, Who created all that is, seen and unseen, taught humanity what it means to be humble. He is a perfect example of humility, a help to overcome pride the cause of the down fall of man. However, man's consolation is the willingness of Jesus to offer assistance, if asked, to overcome every vice. Whatever one does should be done to the Glory of God who has generously bestowed man with His Goodness. One can find God only with humility and patience.

The world today is in a mess. It is only a return to the Creator, the acknowledgement we have failed and need His Help is the way to escape the catastrophe into which the politicians are steering our world. Riots, demonstrations, unrest, wars, sea of refugees, seem to be the order of the day. The mass majority of people in these troubled areas are fed up with their governments, agitating for a change in the ruling class for a better and fair treatment in the distribution of the common good, the wealth of the nation, to reach the less favored and eradicate woeful poverty. It is astonishing, watching the rulers of these countries turn peaceful demonstration into aggression, demonstrating their power with the use of deadly weapons to exterminate innocent lives in order to remain in power. They want to rule at all cost, giving a deaf ear to the demands of their subjects for a change. It takes a man to accept his weakness and face the consequence. A coward, according to Shakespeare, dies many times before his death. The trouble with these leaders who are destroying innocent lives for their political ambition is nothing but pride rooted in self-esteem. How is it possible that someone could be so drowned in ego, in political power, in self-esteem, so blind, so daft, even at the risk of perdition. Why is it impossible for someone, created in the image of God, not to realize the fruits he bears are evil. He has rejected God and chosen evil. God is Love, who is of God bears fruits of love. Does not common sense testify to someone when his actions deviate from goodness to evil?

The truth is, such personalities have sold their souls to Satan which accounts to the hardness of their hearts and their blindness to the injury they cause their fellow human beings. They do to others what they would not want done to them. If such people, who have sold their conscience, on their own free-will, should continue in their wicked ways, paying no heed to the precepts of the God of Creation who loves them, they should bear on mind, failure to reciprocate God's Love and stop evil, they cannot escape His judgement therefore, they should be prepared to face the ultimate consequence of perdition on their departure to eternity when they would stand before the judgement seat of God to account for their evil activities. This very God you so daringly, without remorse, so heartlessly trouble, is your Father, your Creator. He is the Author and Giver of Life. The Creator of all that is, seen and unseen and He loves you infinitely. Despite your wickedness He still loves you and wants to give you life. He will always love you because love is His nature. He beckons you and wants you to return to Him and flee from death, from Satan, the ugly and smelly deceiver. Our good God is a patient God, very long suffering. Your life is in His Hands. It is His Love that sustains you. How would you remain in power O man, if your life is demanded of you? According to Shakespeare, the world is a stage and everyone but a mere player. Everyone plays his part and is heard no more. But there is a difference between one who trusts in the treasures of this world and one whose treasure is in Heaven. The wise put their trust in Jesus Christ while fools put theirs in pomp and riches of this world.

Someone asked Jesus to intervene between him and his brother over their inheritance "bid my brother divide the inheritance with me" and Jesus replied, "Man who made me a judge or a divider over you?" "Take heed, and beware of all covetousness; for a man's life does not consist in the abundance of his possessions" Then he told them a parable "The land of a rich man brought forth plentifully; and he thought to himself, 'What shall I do, for I have nowhere to store my crops?' And he said, 'I will do this: I will pull down my barns, and build larger ones; and there I will store all my grain and my good. And I will say to my soul, Soul, you have ample goods laid up for many years, take your ease, eat, drink, be merry.' But God said to him, 'Fool! This night your soul is required of you; and the things you have prepared, whose will they be?' So is he who lays up treasure for himself and is not rich toward God" This could equally be the fate of all these power-stricken leaders who are so drunk with power, so much so as to liquidate innocent lives without conscience. God stares everyone in the eyes and He knows the secret of the heart. It is either one accepts His Divine Mercy and refrains from wickedness with genuine repentance or face His Judgement. Fortunately, the option is left to one as it is not God's Holy Will for anyone to end up in perdition, therefore the choice is entirely left to each individual.

CHAPTER IX

COMPLETE DELIVERANCE

The most disheartening reality is the blindness of those who have locked up the door of their hearts to the most loving of fathers, to the best Father, to a perfect Father, to the Almighty Father who loves humanity with an infinite love. Who is constantly yearning and beckoning His estranged children to return to Him. A Father from whom humanity exists, a Father who would stop at nothing for the happiness of His Beloved Children. A Father who did not spare the Life of His only begotten Son, gave Him in sacrifice to reunite Himself with humanity and have them share His Divine Life with Him. A Father who did not forget humanity despite their sinfulness, but rather made His only Son pay the wages of their sin, a bitter painful price. All He asks for is that He be trusted. My heart is grieved, for my Father sheds Holy Tears for His children who turn their backs on Him, children who give a deaf ear to His warnings, who would land in perdition. Jesus Christ, Son of God and Son of Virgin Mary, God and Man, lives. He is alive and He makes Himself known to all who sincerely seek Him. He stands at the door of your heart and knocks, let Him in and live. Have pity on Him who loves you infinitely, who is desperately waiting for a reciprocal of His Divine Love for you.

I was most unfortunate to fall into the trap of Satan and came in contact with his agent who tried all he could to pull me into his secret circle, but my Beloved Heavenly Father was patiently watching and waiting for the right time to step forward and pull me out of it so I can live the life He created me to live. I am very proud of my Heavenly Father who did not abandon me, His child, His little Mary of the Most Sacred Heart of

Jesus, and granted me complete deliverance from the pit of hell when He snatched me out of the grip of Satan's agent. It was not an easy experience to be attacked by Satan through his agents, but Our Heavenly Father is Almighty, All powerful, a very loving and protective Father. When it comes to it He proves Himself. Being the loving Father that He is He granted me the Grace to have trust and reach out to Him whenever the agents of darkness made their move. On one such occasion, about 1: 30 am I heard someone coming slowly on a walking stick, I was not sure if it was in my apartment, but it called to mind a similar event which took place in my home town in Nigeria, that incident is narrated fully in my book "Loving God", as the sound drew nearer I realized it was in my apartment and it was the same as in my home town when I was nearly choked, by demonic attack, with a bone of fish, the Lord saw me out of it. This time, as it drew nearer I said to Jesus "my Lord what is that? in a very confidential tone, without fear, in that very second it stopped. I slept soundly in the Arms of Jesus. Jesus is my best friend, a very faithful and trustworthy friend. He is my priceless Treasure, very precious, my Prince charming. I cannot live without Him.

Frankly speaking the Father's Love overwhelms me. He is indeed what He says He is, the best Father. It is advisable to develop a personal relationship with Him in Jesus. Jesus said we should have no fear. We should tell Him all our needs and allow Him to take care of them. The problem with us is impatient and lack of trust. There is nothing to it but prayer, constant prayer is constant contact with the Father, with Jesus and of course with our Mother the Blessed Virgin who protects us with her motherly love, obtaining for us, easily, the graces we desire from her Divine Son. In the book "Loving God" I wrote about the daughter, Antonia, I disowned, the circumstances which led to it, also about her daughter Grace. Now I have also given up Grace. I had thought she could be helped with prayer, but unfortunately I discovered she too has evil influence. Her resentment to my getting deeply involved with Jesus was baffling. To satisfy her resentment she made living together with her hell. Each time I prayed for her I experienced a nightmare, Satanic attacks, thereby ruining my day. Instead of getting better she became worse. My prayers returned back to me empty. It was baffling, whenever I thought of her as family I would have a nightmare. However, the Lord Jesus has taken care of the situation and sent her out of my life. On 01.08.13, I had the nightmare that broke the camel's back which instigated my decision she is no more family. I saw the light in the room hanging on a corner instead of on the usual place in the middle of the room and shaking, in a slow movement. It was very eerie. Then I saw Grace in a corner pretending to be doing something. But when I drew her attention to the light it vanished. Instead, in the same dream, the ventilator in the living-room began blowing fiercely while she watched as though nothing was happening, immediately I began to say the Divine Mercy prayer. St. Paul said, we are not "contending against flesh and blood, but against the principalities, against the powers, against the world rulers of this present darkness, against the spiritual hosts of wickedness in the heavenly places", Eph. 6 : 12 , therefore, we must put on the amour of God which is prayer in order to withstand the wiles of the devil. Prayer is very useful even in dream. However, despite all her mischievousness, all the wrong she did me, making life unbearable for me who is her benefactor, I bear her no grudges. I have forgiven her but I have nothing to do with her any longer hence she has chosen evil on her own free-will.

Someone who knows something is evil and derives pleasure in doing evil is not of God. Such a one has no share in God unless he renounces evil and chooses God. To associate with such a one, being fully aware of his wicked disposition, is taking sides with the enemy of God. It did not matter if that someone is your family member, as long as he refuses to renounce Satan, therefore, any further association with such a person is a setback to one's relationship with Jesus. One cannot serve God and mammon. Besides, one cannot love God haphazardly, one must give his all. Grace is responsible for what becomes of her soul. God's Love is for all including those who hate Him. God is a patient God, God is Love and He loves humanity. His Arms are open to receive every repentant sinner, including Satan's agent who renounces Satan and turns to Him, otherwise he makes himself an enemy of God his Father by choosing to serve Satan with his own will. However, I am grateful to God for the grace to bear her absence and the grace to forgive her. From the age of four she came from Nigeria to live with me, although there was some odd behavior in her then, which I took for granted she would, with time, outgrow, but it turned out I was wrong. At the age of sixteen she had to go when all efforts failed. As I love all that Jesus loves and hate all that He hates, I love everyone both those who hate me because Jesus loves them, but if I knew someone is willfully Satan's agent, aware of God's Mercy yet takes sides with the enemy, I have nothing to do with such a one and everything that belongs to him or her for choosing God's enemy. I renounce evil in all its form. I live with Jesus, Dad and Mary, the Holy Angels watch over us. I am grateful for the relationship I have with Jesus. God's Love is freedom, peace and very fulfilling.

Having had several demonic attacks instigated by his agent, from whom God, out of His infinite Goodness separated me, I decided to go into a dry fasting prayer for seven days for the liberation of my sons. God gave them to me as children of consolation. They were an oasis in the desert of wickedness, under the tutelage of the agent of Satan. The Satan's agent, who had a stroke, used his disableness to deceive my sons. He used it as a means to win their sympathy, making it impossible for them to realize the evil in him. They could not understand that his pretended friendliness was merely a camouflage to prevent them from believing my account of his demonic attacks on my person. He was a tyrant before his stroke, now my sons forgave him believing in his pretended friendliness which made them regard me as heartless, incapable of forgiveness. Little did they know I bore him no grudge for giving me a dog's life, but I had no accommodation in my life for anyone who willfully chose side with the enemy of God. Moreover, my sons began to regard me as somewhat insane due to the transformation our Lord Jesus Christ made in me, having nailed self on His Holy Cross for love of Him. Jesus protected and shielded me from his demonic attacks which he carried out against me when he realized I have come behind his secret. His demonic attacks increased from the disabled home where he landed himself while trying to force me out of the apartment. He fell into his pit. We have a very loving God who grants everyone enough opportunity to turn around and accept His Divine Mercy. God granted him a long rope to renounce Satan but he never did. He knew the bible very well which he used as a camouflage for his evil practices. I tried, having been raised up in a God-fearing home, without bothering about the dog's life he gave me, to pray for him, but each time I did he attacked me with his demonic devices, so I ceased from praying for him. I then began to pray to be set free from his demonic attacks at the same time praying for the deliverance of my sons. Shortly, after a second stroke, he died.

Having come out of his spell due to God's Mercy I put all my trust in God believing He will surely vindicate me and grant my sons the grace to know the truth about the man they called father. I could not fathom the thought he was their father, therefore, to me he was not their father. With a good conscience and trust in God, for me, Jesus is their Father as I am His Bride. I am only their care-taker, the Blessed Virgin Mary, my Mum is their Mother. I believed God would filter every wicked blood out of their veins. "for I the Lord your God am a jealous God, visiting the iniquity of the fathers upon the children to the third and the fourth generation of those who hate me, but showing steadfast love to thousands of those who love me and keep my commandments" God is always the same. I love my sons, Emmanuel and Peter. I desire them to make Heaven. They did not have a happy childhood. I was not in the position to help them as I could not even help myself, therefore, the happiness they lack in this world I desire for them in Heaven. They were brought up in sin, only Jesus can put back the clock and set things straight, so I placed them before the Mercy seat of God for they are not in the position to help themselves as they are brainwashed and blinded by Satan and his agent. However, at the man's death I did not want the boys to go for his burial, if at all they should not go with my two little grandchildren, from Emmanuel my elder son. Unfortunately, they did not regard my words believing me not to be normal. Little did they know that while they were sympathizing with him at the disabled home he was attacking me demonically, appearing to me in the dream in his wickedness. This time, though, he could do nothing. Our Lord Jesus would not let him. I was only made to know, despite his disability he had made his choice to die as Satan's agent.

However, after his burial, my younger son, Peter, visited me with my grandchildren who surprised me with their resentment. All attempts to get them relaxed with me and feel at home was to no avail. Immediately I knew something was wrong. Consequently I commented "I know why"

Emmanuel who was on phone with Peter asked, out of curiosity, to know my reason for such a comment, not desiring him to be upset, I simply told him his children did not see me for a while so that could probably account for their behavior. Having had a foreknowledge something was likely to go wrong, I asked them not to go with the children to the burial, but they would not listen. Thereafter, Peter ate some pistazia from the one I was eating, surprisingly, I had a nightmare that night which never before happened if I ate in the same plate with any of my children. I used to be quite comfortable with my sons and grandchildren whenever they visited me. The dead agent of the evil spirit appeared naked, lying on his back, crawling towards me and I woke up. Out of God's Mercy I was made to realize my sons and my two grandchildren needed prayer of deliverance for the wicked blood to be filtered out from their veins. That gave rise to the seven days dry fasting remembering what Jesus said, some things need fasting and prayer. This was for their salvation and for a normal life. The Lord answered my prayer and I began to wait for the sign I asked of God so as to give testimony in the congregation of His Goodness towards me and mine. He surely will, He is faithful and merciful.

There is nothing most comforting, most soothing, most assuring, most sweet as the love of God. One is in perfect tranquility and one is very secure. To put one's trust in God is a gift of the Holy Spirit and everyone should aspire and pray for it. God is Love and Merciful and He is always willing to grant us every grace for a union with Him. All there is to it is a sincere desire and a surrender to His Holy Will. I cannot be grateful enough to the Lord Jesus Christ for my good relationship with God the Father whom I adore, admire and love with the heart and mind of a child.

Sometimes, the Lord plays with me the way a father plays with his child in reality. Therefore, this being the case, when I saw in my dream a slim red snake, taking it for granted the Heavenly Father was training me to trust in His Fatherly Love and protection, to overcome fear, I reached out for the snake and realized, on stretching it out, it was not a real snake. Then suddenly the light went off and I reached out for the switch to put it on again but was prevented from doing so. Having confidence in God I did not allow it to bother me but went back to bed to continue sleeping.

To my utter surprise a black shadow began pulling on the eiderdown to lie down beside me and I pushed it away and woke up. Consequently, I decided to go into dry fasting for a day for complete deliverance and the Lord answered me through the intercession of the late Vietnamese cardinal Nguyen van Thuan, who will soon be canonized, standing by me while my heavy burden, inform of heavy stones, were being carried by some Vietnamese, I presume Angels, and thrown into a very deep pit down below. Finally, the last one was carried by three of them and thrown into the pit. This shows the universality of the family of God. The saints intercede continuously for us. We are fortunate to be Catholics, to belong in the one Holy Catholic and Apostolic Church founded by Jesus. It is a fortune to belong to His mystical body the Church and to keep His commandments. God is a faithful God. Jesus never fails. We need to be patient with Him and trust in Him.

Another confirmation of my deliverance was when Anthony, the agent of the evil spirit, appeared in another dream, lying down naked, but as I wanted to lie down in front of him for him to hold me, he resented me, although he had always wanted this opportunity. He turned his back to me and moved away from me. On waking up I was very happy and thanked God for His infinite Mercy. The Lord revealed to me my prayer has been answered, the enemy has been defeated and that He, my Father, the Almighty God, who is my Refuge protects me. I am under His Shadow. There is no Father like God. He is my Hero and I love Him. If God be with me who can be against me? I am most fortunate to be the Father's "Little Mary of the Most Sacred Heart of Jesus"

On 06.09.13 I travelled to Dusseldorf in a group of some fellow Catholic Christians for the celebration of the feast of our Lady "Mother of all nations" Just as it is my custom, I never travel without a fasting prayer to commend myself into the Hands of the Almighty Father. Having been raining all week, without desiring to drive home at night, I asked God to choose the bus and the driver, at the same time asking for His Holy Angels to drive the bus for us. I asked Him also to find in the city a parking space for our car – the car belongs to Jesus and me – and to allow His Holy Angels to watch over the car for the three days we would be in Dusseldorf. I must mention here I never make any fasting prayer without Our Blessed Mother. Mum always assists me. The Lord always hears prayers especially when the prayer is made with Mum's assistance. To my complete delight my wonderful Heavenly Father provided a bus for us. To the surprise of the organizer who asked for and paid for a luxurious bus, a smaller bus without an air condition, no toilet, driven by a black driver, on his virgin drive, was sent to us. While others were complaining, the lady organizer weeping, due to the disappointment,

I knew at once it was the Holy Will of our Heavenly Father. I did my best to calm down the lady organizer, telling her she did her best, it was God's Will, we should rather offer our discomfort to the Lord Jesus. To show how wonderful and sweet our Heavenly Father is He gave us a very good weather and our trip was a success. The Lord brought us safely back to Hamburg earlier than expected without much traffic jam. Happily our car was well protected and when I reached home he provided also a packing space in front of the apartment house. As I just drove in a lady drove out as though she was waiting for my arrival.

That notwithstanding, during the celebration of our Lady "Mother of all Nations" in Dusseldorf, on Saturday, 08.09.13, the hall was full for the Adoration, but our dear Lord kept a seat for me exactly where He would pass during the procession. Oh how I felt my Dad was passing by and wanted to feel His Presence, and felt nothing. He passed three times, and each time I wanted to feel Him but to no avail. However, I knew He was aware of me, He noticed me and knew exactly my intentions. A loving Father never passes his child by without taking notice of him and God, my Father, the best Father why would He not notice me His little girl, His "little Mary of the Most Sacred Heart of Jesus". But He did. Having surrendered myself totally to our Lord Jesus Christ, loving all that He loves and hating all that He hates, I am fully aware He has turned His back on Anthony who, on his own free-will, chose to serve Satan the enemy of God, rejecting all the opportunities God offered him to turn back to Him, I reject also everything and anything associated with him. For this reason, having had a bad experience in what was revealed to me in the dream, after asking my sons not to attend his burial and they paid no heed to it, I found it difficult to embrace them any longer until they renounce every emotional attachment to Anthony and embrace Jesus fully. The boys have not known what it is to live and they do not know their direction. They are not aware Anthony used evil device to block their success in life. I know about this due to God's Mercy. Although my elder son threatened to break away from the Catholic Church I was not affected by his threats because I know what instigated him to say such a thing, besides I have confidence in God. I know also, should they fall dead, God would raise them up until they are freed from the filthy blood of Anthony, the agent of Satan, enemy of God. To fall in love with God who is always faithful, and aiming at keeping His precepts is a great favor from God.

Bearing this on mind, to my utter surprise on Monday morning, the day after we came back from Dusseldorf, having prepared as usual, to go to the church and spend some time with my Beloved in the tabernacle, I did not know why I could not move from home as early as I planned, even though I was ready. Somehow, immediately after praying, the doorbell rang. I am not in the habit of opening the door without prior notice, I asked Jesus for the assurance to open the door, being under His Personal protection. To my utter surprise, it was my sons and they pleaded with me to open the door for them informing me their name has been changed. Again I informed Jesus, on receiving His permission, confidently, I opened the main gate for them. It was a happy surprise from God the Father. He knows how I miss them and long to see them. The boys who usually took offence, talking like parrots if they did not understand something, were calm, quite unlike their usual behavior. They lacked the ability to listen calmly for an explanation if they misunderstood something, a bad habit to which they were exposed in their childhood by Anthony who was himself a bundle of temper and a talkative. I discovered we could discuss without friction, and laughed together. The information about the application to change their identity was a source of joy to me which increased my hope for their happiness and success in life, knowing fully well the damage and the evil influence Anthony's name has had in their life. Although I did not allow them into the apartment they quite understood. Happily I thanked the Lord Jesus for this wonderful surprise, the reason I did not feel His presence as He passed me by during the procession.

The fact our Lord Jesus made them come so I could at least see them and know all is well with them was a blessing. The Lord has started His work on the boys and this work, by His grace, He will accomplish in due course as I have absolute confidence in Him. Mary, my sweet loving Mum will always intercede and cover Her children with Her cloak. Perhaps, it would be interesting to mention my elder son was almost killed, had it not been for God's Mercy. I was not surprised, the enemy always dares, but God always protects His children. This time, due to the attempt to change his name, Anthony mobilized his master Satan, and sent the police to search my son Emmanuel, someone born in Germany who has never had such control from the police, was almost strangled to death by the police at the police station where they sprayed gas at him. An unusual and absurd attitude on the part of the police because he gave them no resistance, rather obediently followed them to the police station. Despite his surprise, not knowing the reason for such a surmon to the police station he made no resistance. Anthony's sole concern was to see the children join him in hell. As long as the boys hang on him emotionally, bearing his name, he would not allow them surrender to Jesus, love God and be saved. Jesus, a faithful God, the best Father and a most compassionate Beloved, Who in His infinite Goodness, gave me victory over Anthony and his wicked plans with Satan, has set the boys free from his wickedness. He chose Satan on his own free-will, therefore the children have no share in it for they are God's children, their place is Heaven.

On the long run, the enemy has lost the battle. God in His infinite Goodness, granted me on 27.12.2014, the grace to witness with my own eyes the victory He gave me over my enemy, Anthony who engaged other wicked people, like himself, in the service of Satan, including two of my neighbors, to achieve his wicked intensions against me, failed because of God's Divine Mercy, His Fatherly Love and protection. God always reveals to me those he uses and their wicked plans. This day, the feast of John the Apostle which is also the Eve of the feast of the Holy Family, there was no Mass in my parish, but as I love the Mass I made some calls to find out where there was to be Mass on that day. Somehow, when I did not get through to the parish of my choice, instinctively I called up the parish I did not intend calling and the priest picked up the phone and informed me there was Mass in his parish, St. Joseph, in the evening at 5 o'clock. However, rather than rejoicing for this opportunity, I felt somewhat reluctant to attend due to the distance of the Church, besides the area, Reeperbahn, is not attractive, an area for the sins from hell, sins of the flesh. Again, 5 o'clock in winter appeared late to me, but somehow I felt it was God's Holy Will that I attend. If one is in tune with God, He always directs one and He has a way of making one realize His Will. As the priest was willing to come earlier to hear my confession I saw it as an opportunity to enter the coming year filled with the Grace of God.

To my surprise, I entered the Church to find only a disabled elderly man sitting alone at the end of the front row with his walking-roller in front of him, on it was the hymnbook. As there was no way I could locate the priest, not being from the parish therefore, instinctively I went to the man to find out from him if the priest had arrived. Surprisingly, the man who held his head up sank his head down, on hearing my voice, and closed his eyes. On touching him he remained motionless like a corpse, my question about the priest unanswered. feeling he must be deaf and dumb I decided to say my prayers first and get myself ready for the Mass. I sat in the third row behind him. When I was done with my prayers, unable to find the hymn book, remembering the disabled had one, seeing his head raised up, his eyes wide open, I went over to him again to know from him where he got the hymnbook. Again to my utter surprise he sank his head down, his eyes closed. I touched him asking about the hymnbook. Again there was no movement and no sound. He was motionless like a corpse. It was awkward, but I gave no further thought to it except to ponder how such a one who could neither speak nor hear could come alone to the Church and wondered how he could participate at Mass.

To my relief, the priest finally arrived as he said he would, got himself ready and I had my confession. Oh, what a wonderful confession! A confession that turned into a blessing. The Lord spoke to me through His priest. It was an absolution coupled with blessing. I was to include those who came to my mind in my confession. I was so happy to include my loved ones. However, I found the hymnbooks which were on a corner close to the confessional as the faithful gradually began streaming into the Church. Surprisingly, when the Mass began the disabled man, who could neither talk nor hear stood up, moved somewhat to his left and began singing louder than every other person dragging the song in a wrong direction. That notwithstanding, it was a wonderful Mass in which I experienced a thrilling union with my Beloved in the Eucharist. As I was about to go I was caught up with a fantastic feeling, while the pianist played, my spirit was uplifted and I was in Heaven filled with the love of God and tremendous joy in my heart with thrills all over my body. Oh how wonderful it is the Word took flesh so we can reach God. The Baby Jesus, God's wonderful gift to humanity. What a wonderful Mystery. I love You my God for being You.

At about 2 am, just before getting up for my morning prayer, I woke up with a dream about Anthony, although I did not see him but his younger brother Andrew with his son. They told me Anthony brought only one fish to which I responded he brought many. However, I felt he brought only one fish, but the many he brought were not seen. When I woke up I could not make out what the dream meant although I know that whenever the Lord reveals something to me before waking up it usually relates to reality, always meaningful. Nevertheless, I decided not to ponder much about it and felt the Lord knows why he gave me such a dream having asked Him to keep me from such dreams as they affect my mood during the day. However, while praying the Lord made known to me the meaning of the dream. It was Anthony I saw in the disabled man in the Church. It was then I realized the resemblance. The attitude of the man was exactly his, whenever he was disinterested in something, but being like a corpse shows he is dead. He died as a disabled man. He tortured me before and after his stroke as disabled, ungrateful for the help I offered him for thirteen years. As an agent of Satan, like his master, his answer to goodness is wickedness. My enemies have been finally defeated. Anthony mobilized many wicked spirits demonically against me to achieve his wicked aims to take me along with him if he died. Now, after his death he intensified his demonic attacks. The many fishes which I knew he came with without seeing are the wicked spirits he utilized for his wicked purposes. His brother whom he used also as an instrument wanted to deceive me with his son but without success because the Spirt of God is in me. The Holy Trinity dwells in me. I am a Child of the Almighty God. The one fish means Anthony was alone in the Church. He could not look at me because he was afraid of me due to the Presence of the Almighty God in me. Me and mine are under the protection of God. I am wearing a shield of the Lord. His Most Precious Blood is my Shield. Our Lord Jesus Christ conquered the powers of darkness. If we trust in Him we realize our victory. I have an unwavering trust in God. With my sweet Bridegroom Jesus I can do anything for Him and in Him. Glory be to God in the highest and on earth peace to men of good will. Me and mine are free at last praise be to God! My God I adore and love thee.

All praise and all thanksgiving be to You O Lord my God. "The Lord works vindication and justice for all who are oppressed .... The Lord is merciful and gracious, slow to anger and abounding in steadfast love..... the steadfast love of the Lord is from everlasting to everlasting upon those who fear him, and his righteousness to children's children, to those who keep his covenant and remember to do his commandments."

The enemy has lost the battle, my sons are free and under the personal protection of our Lord Jesus Christ and Mary our blessed Mother. Prior to this visual experience of my complete deliverance, granted to me and mine by the Almighty Father, the Lord granted me, after a day fasting prayer, a beautiful dream in which there was a celebration and the good Lord granted me the grace to dance with my father who, due to His infinite Mercy, I was made to know is by Him in Heaven. It was a dance of celebration for the salvation of my sons, the deliverance from all evil. Being under the protection of the two Hearts of Love is to be completely secure. If God be for us who can be against us? The Lord Jesus is faithful, I have absolute trust in Him and I am head over heels in love with Him. His Holy Will is my delight and His Happiness my priority.

CHAPTER X

TOTAL SURRENDER TO GOD'S LOVE

To fall in love with God is to be alive. There is nothing more intoxicating, more refreshing, more sweet as God's love. God's Love is Heaven on earth. Humanity searches for love, peace and tranquility in places of transient, with transitory means, whereas the Almighty Father Who is Love, manifested His Infinite Love to humanity by offering humanity His only Begotten Son who is Love. The key to happiness is Jesus Christ, the only begotten Son of the Father, Son of God and Son of Virgin Mary, truly God and truly Man. To experience peace and tranquility in perfect love is total surrender to God the Father in Jesus Christ through Mary. One cannot love Jesus Christ without loving Mary His Beloved Mother whom He loves above all being, the Mother of the family of God, of the new Israel. The two Hearts of Love, the Sacred Heart of Jesus and the Immaculate Heart of Mary are perfectly united, they are entwined and cannot be separated. They are to be loved together, though Jesus as God, the Father of all Creation, hence there is only one true God. Jesus embodies the Eternal Father and the Holy Spirit. He is the only Son of the Almighty God, Brother, Friend and Redeemer of humanity. Mary is to be loved, under other Titles, as the Mother of Jesus the Redeemer, the Word Incarnate, Mother of humanity, of all nations, Mother of God, of the new Israel, Mother of the Family of God in Heaven and on Earth, the Church. Jesus cannot be your brother if you did not accept His Mother as your Mother. Christianity is based on Faith and Faith is a gift of the Holy Spirit. So pray for the virtue of Faith and Fortitude to enable you put Faith into practice as the Bible says "Faith without work is dead".

The best source of Faith is prayer to enable you obtain Faith in Jesus in the Eucharist, Who transforms us into His Divine Self, if received always in a state of grace. The none Catholics who receive Jesus as symbol, in the Communion, cannot, beyond doubt, have a real personal relationship with Him. Being outside His Mystical Body, the Church, the One Holy Catholic and Apostolic Church He founded Himself, equipped her with seven Sacraments for the sanctification of the soul, is an impediment for a true personal relationship with Him. One cannot have a real relationship with someone one does not have, with someone not fully known. Jesus is in the Holy Eucharist, Body, Blood, Soul and Divinity. Catholics therefore, who know their Faith well and live their Faith are indeed in Heaven on Earth. It is not adequate to be Catholic, receive Jesus in the Eucharist on regular basis, without actually opening the door of the heart to the Beloved Redeemer. One does not have to remain in sin that grace may abound, so to say, first sin and then afterwards go to confession. Jesus did not institute the Sacrament of Reconciliation for one to indulge in sin and become a swine. He, who is Love and hates sin does not reside in such hearts where He is scourged and crowned with thorns all over again. If God our Father is Love we also should be love to resemble Him who created us in His own image. It is only in love for one another and for neighbor, "Love ye one another as I have loved you," one experiences the Father's love and becomes prepared to embrace the Cross in all its forms, as charity becomes the emblem of victory against the wiles of the enemy, under the perfect protection of the Most Precious Blood of the Most Loving God, Jesus Christ our Beloved Redeemer. His Most Sacred Heart becomes a Refuge in the ocean of his Divine Mercy. The meaning of the Cross would be understood, the persistent effort of the enemy to create, on the mind, a wrong impression of it would be to no avail. It would be a slap on his face, having been defeated by the very means he used for his victory over Adam and Eve.

The love of one's neighbor is generated by the love in one's heart for God. The inability of expressing love to everyone, to all God's children originates from lack of love for God, a disease of the soul which requires an urgent cure. It is not enough to love special people and recent others. The whole of humanity are children of God infinitely loved by Him. A soul incapable of love has no place in Heaven. Heaven is Jesus Christ and Jesus Christ is Love therefore, He alone is the cure for a sick soul and the key to His Heart of Love is humility. My sympathy goes to souls under the tutelage of the enemy the Satan, who allow their minds to be governed by him, to be a playground of manipulation, the seat of darkness that eventually would lead them to perdition, as it causes them reject the Light, Jesus Christ who is eternal Life. However, more so do I sympathize with those souls who say they are in the Light, yet are very lonely souls who receive Jesus in the Eucharist, yet, possess the symptoms of sick souls. Such are aggressive, easily irritated, uncheerful, complainants, antagonistic, unforgiving people, to mention but a few. How could there be a reflection of Jesus in such souls, how could they bear witness to God's Love if their souls are wanting in love.

It was a surprise to hear someone who receives Jesus regularly in the Eucharist, attends retreats, respond to her fellow sister in Christ who cheerfully said to her, as she offered her a helping hand, "My sister let me help you" feeling sympathy for the heavy shopping bags she had to carry, only to get the response "I am not your sister you irritate me" This unfortunate Catholic Christian, though she receives Jesus regularly, failed to realize, in high opinion of herself, she shut the door of her heart to Jesus and comes short of God's grace. Someone who reacts negatively, without enthusiasm or openness to loving sisterly or brotherly conversation about our Faith, about to the love of God, is completely incapable of attaining a closer and genuine relationship with Jesus. How would someone deficient in love, in humility, who exhibits the notion of being instructed on what she already knows – pride – appreciate love from a cheerful, innocent and helpful sister with whom she is supposed to live together in Heaven with Jesus. Without love one has no chance of Heaven. When the heart is focused on Heaven, no amount of sacrifice is too much. Anything would be tolerated and endured through God's grace for the love of Jesus. Such souls, with intricate character, deserve sympathy and commendation to God in prayer who alone can heal souls with His Divine grace. A regular examination of self and frequent reception of the Sacrament of Reconciliation are important if Heaven is the focus for Divine grace to overcome the perils and trials of our time.

Oh Dear Sweet Love, God my Father, infinite Goodness, possess me, mold me, transform me into Mercy, perfect me in Charity, that I be Love and Mercy as You Father, like Jesus and Mary. Oh that the daughter maybe Love even as the Father is Love. Your little Mary of the Most Sacred Heart of Jesus, Your Princess, Your Child.

May You have delight in me when you look at me. Infuse in me Dad, Mum's Virtues that I may resemble Her, resemble Jesus, Your Divine Son and be like You. Purify me like gold. Oh that I may resemble the Family, Dad Dearest. May the time left for me in this exile, Oh Most Merciful Dad, be useful to You.

Oh my Dearest, Sweet Beloved Heavenly Father, How I look forward to the end of my exile here below to be eternally with You there, up in Heaven to rest on Your Most Beautiful, Most Loving, Most Wonderful Fatherly Bosom and be pampered by You with Your Fatherly Love, that I may love You eternally as Your darling daughter, praising You with Your Holy Angels and Saints throughout Eternity, beholding Your Beauty.

What sadness fills my soul, contemplating the Heavenly Father's pain for his estranged children, especially the atheists, who deny His existence and have not experienced His Love. If only they would realize the great tenderness and sweetness of the Father's infinite Love for them they would regret all their life for having ever turned their back on Him causing Him so much pain. The Father created us in His own image, part of Him in us should enable us realize His existence. Humanity is endowed with intellect and the whole of creation is at our disposal to enable us wonder, search and find the most wonderful God of creation, the most loving Father of humanity. Jesus stands at the door of every heart and knocks, waiting to be ushered in in order to lead one to the Father. Have sympathy for Jesus who has sacrificed His Life for love of you. Make hay while the sun shines, when Jesus is patiently beckoning you to return to Him, to the Father whose desire is to shower you with His fatherly Love and save you from damnation. As the soul is immortal and the ultimate fate of the soul is either damnation or eternal life with Jesus, in Him and for Him in Eternity, there is an urgent need for a well thought decision in this exile world how one wishes to spend eternity eternally. The choice is left for every individual. Everyone has the liberty of benefiting now from His Divine Mercy before it is too late.

How beautiful it is to swim in the ocean of Divine Mercy and be enveloped by Divine Love. Oh how beautiful and sweet is Divine Love. To be under the personal protection of the Almighty God, our Eternal Father, guarantees a wonderful security as one takes refuge in the Most Sacred Heart of Jesus through Mary our sweet Mother. Sincerely speaking, I am most fortunate to be the daughter of God, to have Mary and Jesus as my Parents, very sweet loving Parents. The most interesting thing is that they are the Parents of everyone. We are God's Family. All you need is to realize this, accept this beautiful fortune of having them as your parents, be subordinate, obedient, humble, believe, trust and open your heart and accommodate them. If God is your Father what could be more natural as to trust and have faith in Him and be in Heaven while on Earth.

There is nothing to be compared with Love. God is Love. I am head over heels in love with Love. To love God is to be in Heaven while on Earth. Having a personal relationship with the Holy Trinity, in Jesus Christ, enables you, in the course of this relationship, to discover yourself. You will then begin to realize you live in this world, yet you are not of this world. Life in this world begins to have a meaning to you which eventually will awaken the desire, the longing for your Eternal Home by the Father where you belong. The Eternal Home where the Father's overwhelming love awaits you. Having surrendered completely to the Father's Love in humble trust the Father takes care of me, instructing me, granting me His Fatherly guidance in my everyday life. In utter humility and content, I appreciate the Divine Mercy for the grace to understand and embrace the cross in any form, depending on the Father's Love, in Jesus Christ, who walks and works with me sharing everything with me, Joys, sorrows, pains and Agony. In love I depend entirely on Jesus and I trust in Him. My place is to serve Him the way He wants me to serve Him, wait patiently for Him and Mum to come for me when my time in this exile is over, to take me to my eternal Home in Heaven to live with Jesus, for Jesus and in Jesus eternally in Eternity. I simply cannot wait for that moment of my departure from this exile, that moment would be the happiest moment of my life in this exile when Jesus, my Darling Sweet Beloved Bridegroom will come with my darling Mum Mary, to take me to the ultimate Bliss of my first union with Jesus, in His Heavenly Palace, when my life begins in Him, with Him and for Him throughout Eternity. Oh, how I look forward to the Resurrection when we will all be in our glorified bodies. Could you imagine what a wonderful life that would be, always with the Beloved eternally throughout Eternity, never ever to be separated from Him again. What a wonderful sweet Vision of Jesus. In fact, to be part of it no sacrifice is too much. If one chooses Life with Jesus and returns Love for love, Jesus grants the grace and the strength to persevere, when asked in humility.

During the month of July, I decided to offer Mum some roses for her assumption into Heaven by meditating on the Rosary decade to that effect, every day nine thousand times, coupled with daily fasting prayer, continuously until the feast of her assumption on 15th August 2013. The fasting prayer was to make my present more attractive, taking nothing until 3 o'clock in the evening. Having made this decision, I began with the prayer on the 1st of August, but to my utter surprise, on that very first day, at about 1:30 am I woke up suddenly from sleep completely overwhelmed with the weakness of our dear Lord Jesus. Normally, it would not have been a surprise to me as He has already blessed me with the grace to share His suffering with Him, but it has never been to this intensity. It was always for some few minutes and each time I would seek the toilette to ease myself, sitting down until the weakness eases off. This usually happens during my morning prayer leaving me wondering at what Jesus had to endure for love of me, how He managed to cope with his passion, the terrible torture He allowed Himself to suffer for the love of humanity. He bore it all at a stretch, different types of pain on His blessed Humanity. He had no room to breathe, from one suffering to the other, until He shed His last drop of Blood on the cross on calvary. However, when I first experienced this weakness, I had no idea what I was suffering from, therefore I sought the help of my doctor, who, unable to discover my ailment, recommended me to a radiologist who had me examined with a computer tomography and found nothing. In due time I realized it was from my Beloved, hence He has already given me the stigmata, five of them, and the thorns which I experienced consecutively at His Will.

Jesus keeps and governs those He won with the strength of His Love. The Almighty God, the Eternal Father always turns bad into good for those who love Him. One day I could not find the cholesterol tablets I used to take, without realizing it was the mischief of Satan, I took it for granted Jesus does not want me to take the tablet any longer. I felt He desired a special relationship with me, a relationship of complete trust in Him as my sweet all and all, the Lord and Giver of Life, the physician of all physicians. Therefore, I gave Him my complete trust in the belief nothing will happen to me unless it is His Holy Will, after all He is the

Lord and Lover of my soul. I belong entirely to Him with delight. Today I do not have need for cholesterol tablets and I eat everything I like eating which I gave up before due to the rise of the cholesterol level.

However, this time the weakness was indeed very severe. It was so intense I did not know initially what was happening to me. All I knew was the immediate urge to seek the toilet. My stomach was filled with much air and aching. To pass gas meant frequent visit to the toilet and each time I let out only water. The situation was so frightening and so pitiably messy as I had frequent change of my panties and lots of usage of hygiene pads. So many possibilities of what might be happening to me flashed on my mind such as cholera, food poisoning, terrified at the very thin faeces, sometimes black and in clumps like that of a goat having traces of blood, and I had fever. To my utter surprise, I felt as though I was left entirely to myself as the Lord Jesus withdrew from me. I could not reach Him any more as I used to, but somehow, I felt He was there only He did not want me to be consciously aware of His Presence in me as usual. The constant presence of the Holy Trinity which feels me with His Love and warmth, despite my unworthiness, I now missed greatly. However, despite all odds, I simply trusted myself into His care and continued my fasting prayer and my Rosary as I promised Mum. But each day, when I closed my fasting prayer, I had no appetite for food. I simply could not bring myself to eat. It became a real burden to eat, then, somehow it dawned on me Jesus was aware of what was happening to me and that it was His handwriting. I realized I was safe in His Hands all I needed to do was to co-operate with Him regardless of all the discomfort. I knew also He was suffering with me, if there was an alternative He would have granted it me because He loves me. In fact He suffered more than I was doing. I felt fortunate to share with Him this little nothing, compared to what He suffered for love of me.

If I did not have a relationship with Jesus, considering the nature of my ailment, I would have rushed to a medical doctor. I was in the habit of seeking a doctor for every little thing. Sometimes only for a checkup as I did not want a surprised ailment. I do not have this need now, I have Jesus the doctor of doctors Who has life. In my relationship with Jesus He is everything to me. I am most fortunate to have a relationship of total surrender to my Beloved Redeemer Who is delighted to be my sweet Everything. The turmoil of my ailment did not affect my daily attendance to Mass. I could drive to attend Mass without disturbance, but as soon as I got back home the dilemma of rushing almost every minute to the toilet began. In the same manner I walked down from my apartment to my parish Church for Mass without problem, no stomach problem until I got back home to experience the dilemma all over again.

Mass is conducted four times a week in my parish, therefore I seek other parishes for Mass. From Monday to Wednesday I drive to three different Churches of some distance from my place of abode. Jesus permitted me to drive to these Churches only and also when I have something to do down town, but to my parish Church I should go on foot, hence it is only a stone throw. This I began happily to cherish and appreciate as I realized the good effect it has on me, at the same time it provides me the opportunity to bring Jesus to those I come across. This paved way for me to evangelize. Bringing Jesus to my estranged brothers and sisters is of great delight to me, an attempt to help wipe the tears in the Beloved Father's eyes, the best Father, full of Love and Mercy. May we hurt Him no more and give Him our hearts. Trusting in our Lord Jesus Christ leads to the discovery of a most loving, wonderful, merciful God who is Love.

During this period of my ailment, which no longer, despite the discomfort, was a dilemma in that sense, but a privilege to suffer for Jesus and with Jesus, having realized it all started exactly on the day I was to begin to give Mum some roses, I decided to bear it all with Jesus. My nourishment and sustenance was the Holy Eucharist. Due to lack of sleep, having to wake up for toilet at night and being unable to fall asleep before the next call to the toilet I asked Jesus to grant me the grace to continue sleeping despite the urge to go to toilet. He granted it me. I could sleep through the night, even though I woke up sometimes with the urge to seek the toilet but I did not heed to it. The whole incident went on for seven days. It all ended early in the morning of 8th August. Although this was a tough experience, I am very grateful to Jesus to have allowed me share in His suffering. My soul magnifies the Lord and my spirit rejoices in God my Savior because He has regarded the lowliness of His handmaid, for behold henceforth I am the Beloved of my God. What a feeling of security one derives in the Love of Jesus. His love fills my heart with peace and tranquility. I am most fortunate Jesus loves me and I believe deep down in my heart nothing will ever happen to me except it be His Holy Will. Although it seemed as though He abandoned me during this period, I am very grateful for the grace to hold on to my trust in Him by remembering all He has done for me, His graces and favors, thanks to St. Ignatius of Loyola and his spiritual exercises. I have absolute confidence in the Love of Jesus for me. He will never abandon me. He is such a wonderful sweet, faithful and trustworthy God. I am happy He created me and loves me infinitely. I love Him. Faith like a mustard seed can indeed move mountain. I asked Jesus to make the Beatitudes part of me and clothe me with the virtues of obedience, humility and purity as I have made His Holy Words my clothing and live on them.

CHAPTER XI

MARY MY MUM

A mother's love is very unique, very special radiating warmth, security, compassion, understanding, tolerance, patience, to name but a few and very soothing to the soul. A mother's love is God's Love. Any mother who is deficient in these attributes is not fit to be called a mother. God loves us with a mother's love infinitely. The beauty of Love is embedded in the attributes of Love, Virtues of God Who is Love and Beauty. Love is sweet and beautiful – God is Love, Beauty, Good, Mercy. Goodness is of Love and only God is good. In our weak human nature there is part of God in us, hence we came from Him and each individual is capable of love, imperfectly though, but this love is enhanced when joined to the Divine Love offered to humanity in Jesus Christ, if accepted, to be perfected in the same Jesus Christ eternally in the Father's Love in Eternity. Then would we live with the Father in Heaven eternally, in perfection, in Eternity. The Saints in Heaven enjoy this perfection, already granted them in Jesus Christ. This beautiful wonderful fortune is made possible for humanity by Jesus Christ with the shedding of His Most Precious Blood.

The Incarnation of the Word, Jesus Christ, truly Man and truly God, in search of that which was lost, portrays the beauty of God's Love for humanity, thereby revealing Him as the best Father in His motherly love for His little souls He created in his own image and clothed with body.

God's perfect parenthood is mirrored in the humble obedience of the Word Incarnate in the total emptying of Himself in His Humanity, His humble acceptance of His Holy Cross, His endurance and obedience to the Will of the Eternal Father even unto death. Despite His for-knowledge of His bitter predicament in the hands of His creatures, the unimaginable terrible pains, physical and mental strains, which depth humanity would never know, which were certainly beyond human endurance, He did not hesitate to take Flesh, an indication of His infinite love and His divine desire for the salvation of man. What a fortune for humanity to be adorned with such an infinite Love, so miserably unworthy though humanity is. This beautiful Love of the Almighty God is perfected in Mary the Mother of Jesus who was Immaculately conceived. Mary, a wonder, the Pride of God, the Crown of His Creation who reflects God's beauty, His priceless Possession, is the wonderful gift to humanity without whom there would have been no Incarnation. Is it not amazingly wonderful and most beautiful and exciting that the Mother of God is the Mother of humanity? What a fortune! Humanity has the same Mother with the God of the Universe, Creator of all that is, seen and unseen. Yes, His Mother is your mother, how wonderful, if only you accept Her. When we love and honor Mary we love, honor and admire God for His merciful Love.

The awareness of this amazing relationship to God generates such joy in my heart that leaves me in complete admiration for God who deems it fit, in His infinite Goodness to call me His sister. Yes, that's exactly what I am, poor wretched creature like me, so unworthy, less than half of an Ant, a Cinderella – Aschenputtel – yet the sister of Jesus Christ my God. Sometimes, my heart is so delighted with joy I feel like flying. Indeed, though I feel so unworthy, I realized I am a princess, the little girl, little Mary of the Most Sacred Heart of Jesus, darling daughter of God the Father, the King of Kings and Lord of Lords and the Queen of Heaven is my Mum. Although I am not recognized as a princess in this exile, it is rightly so, for my Mum and my Dad know I am one, hence I am their little girl, their little Mary of the Most Sacred Heart of Jesus. You might not believe it, but it is true, Mum tucks me lovingly into the Arms of Jesus while I rest my weary head on His Blessed Chest and sleep peacefully and soundly like a new born baby and wake up in the morning refreshed to give thanks and praises to the Almighty Father for being such a wonderful sweet loving Dad. With so much love from my heavenly Parents here in this exile, I cannot wait to embrace them in Heaven and enjoy their love fully in Heavenly Bliss. To be pampered by my heavenly Father with His Fatherly Love and be doted on by my heavenly Mum with her motherly love in Heaven is my great desire. However, I need to exercise patience until the Father calls me Home. Meanwhile, by His Grace and according to His Holy Will, it is my place to protect His interest here in this exile, for Jesus, my sweet Beloved, to fight for my Father's Kingdom as I should. My deepest desire being to spend Eternity in Heaven with Jesus eternally, I asked Him for the Grace to abide in His Love with my focus always on Him. Jesus is my Hope and my Heaven, for His Love no suffering is too much. He grants the Grace for it. The greatest security for one's soul is Jesus. However, to obtain this security is to trust in Him, abide in His Love and persevere. One way to abide in His Love is to love His Mother.

Oh what a wonderful act of Love from Jesus to give humanity His Mother. Mum's motherly love for me portrays God's Love for me who loves me with a motherly love. There is nothing like a mother's love and Mum is perfected in Love and she is always there whenever she is needed, showering me with her motherly love and drawing me closer to her Divine Son. She is my teacher and guide, my model, I love to emulate her because I love her and much more I love Her Divine Son. Besides, she is my girlfriend. Probably, I must have mentioned this earlier, Mary my Mum is to me as though she were my biological mum and so do I relate to her, so much so, that she even lends me her assistance whenever I am in dire need of it, even in very simple everyday life, like in bottoming and unbuttoning my skirt at the back in my incapability to do so. In fact this close relationship between Mum and me is God' grace. She is such a loving Mum and I love her very very very dearly. I simply feel sorry for those who do not love her and yet claim to love her Son, but this cannot be true love. How could one love the Son and reject the Mother. To love Jesus is to love Mary. When people said to Jesus "Your mother and your brethren are standing outside desiring to see you" Jesus said to them "My mother and my brethren are those who hear the word of God and do it" Lk 8 vs 20, 21. This has been wrongly interpreted by protestant Christians having caught themselves off from the Vine. The Church, which is the Body of Christ, the One, Holy, Catholic and Apostolic Church, has been given to know the secret of the Kingdom of God, therefore She has the whole Truth and She only can explain the Bible because Her Soul is the Holy Spirit. "To you it has been given to know the secret of the kingdom of God: but for others they are in parables, so that seeing they may not see, and hearing they may not understand" Lk 8 vs 10. What Jesus tries to state clearly here is simply the necessity to be obedient to the word of God, to emulate Mary in her obedience to God even though she did not understand, she trusted in God's love for her.

"Behold I am the handmaid of the Lord, be it done unto me according to your word" This simple genuine statement portraying a total giving of self to the Divine Will of God in humble trust is indeed more than admirable, at such a tender age, with such innocence. She is indeed unexampled. Besides, Mary is the new Eve, therefore Jesus called Her "Woman" just as Adam called Eve "Woman." "The woman beguiled me and I did eat" In the same way Jesus called Mary "Woman" at the wedding at Cana and on the Cross when He gave Her to the Beloved disciple John because She is the Mother of humanity, of the Family of God in the new Covenant, the Mother of the Church. Mary has no rival in obedience to the Word of God. Having been chosen and fashioned for God's Divine purpose in the salvation of humanity she proved herself, despite the tenderness of her youth, equal to the task for which she was chosen. Her complete surrender to God's Holy Will in humble trust, "be it done to me according to thy word" though she did not understand, but pondered in her heart, so also the sword that pierced her heart as she suffered in her Immaculate heart the bitter passion of her Divine Son, suffering together with Him the abandonment of the Eternal Father "my God, my God, why hast thou forsaken me?" paved way for her eminent role, as a co-redemptrix in the salvation of humanity by her Divine Son. There at the foot of the cross, despite "Woman behold your son, son behold your mother" under terrible labor she bore the new Israel, the Church, when the soldier's lance pierced the Sacred Side of Her Divine Son, wounded his sacred Heart and blood and water gushed out from His Sacred Side as a fount of Mercy for the world.

Jesus began at the instance of His conception to suffer for the redemption of humanity and so did Mary His Mother. Had the Angel not revealed to Joseph, Her betrothal, the Baby in Her womb was by the Holy Spirit, She and Her Son would have been sent away secretly by Joseph, a righteous man, to save Her from being stoned to death to an unknown fate. That notwithstanding, What did She get to hear at the presentation of Her Son in the Temple of Jerusalem, an occasion of great joy for every mother, "Behold, this child is set for the fall and rising of many in Israel, and for a sign that is spoken against (and a sword will pierce through your own soul also) that the thoughts out of many hearts may be revealed." From that instance Her Heart was fixed with a sword. Mary's unique position in the salvation history is Her faith and trust in Her Divine Son till the end. When both Heaven and Earth, God and humanity turned against Him Mary stood by Him. She never doubted Him. How could God's Son go through that terrible passion, subject Himself to a torture never before heard of, mockery and humiliation in silence? Could it be He is not really what He said He is? A whole nation against Her Son and every finger pointing at Her as the Mother of Him Who is a Cheat, an Impostor, a blasphemer, yet she kept calm and stood by Him at the foot of the cross, suffering with Him in her Heart. All His shame was Hers, the numerous wounds on His delicate Skin caused by the sadistic scourgers were a nightmare as she beheld what became of Her Baby, the most beautiful Son in the whole wide world and Her Immaculate Heart sank in deep sorrow. There was no healthy spot on His Body including the soles of His feet, part of his flesh torn to such extent that the ribs were exposed. How Her Immaculate Heart fevered and bled as Her Divine Son was nailed to the cross, His limbs straightened and dislocated. Every blow of the executioner's hammer felt in Her Immaculate Heart. How helpless She felt in the midst of their enemy, no one to help Her Son nor could she help Him. She suffered in silence like Her Son. Sorrow was too great an unwelcomed visitor that would have caused Her death had God not sustained Her.

Mary was not just a figure head, she played an active role in the salvation of humanity. It pleases God humanity should honor Her as She herself said in the magnificent "For Behold, henceforth, all generations shall call me blessed". She deserves every honor. She is a Jewel of great price for humanity because through Her all humanity became brothers and sisters of Jesus Christ. To reject Mary is to reject Jesus. Jesus is God. He is truly God and truly Man. If Jesus is truly God and truly Man then Mary is the Mother of God. Jesus Himself calls Her, even today, His Mother. God the Son and God the Father are one. Jesus said it. "Whoever has seen me has seen the Father" "The Father is in me and I am in the Father" Mary is the mother of the new covenant, the new Israel. Mother of all nations. I deem myself fortunate to have Her as my mother, what about you?" She is the gate of Heaven. Yes, believe in the Lord Jesus Christ and you will be saved. That is quite right, but to believe in the Lord Jesus Christ means to believe in what He stands for. To observe His commandments. He gave His Mother to us on the Cross when He said to the beloved Apostle "Son behold your mother" The rejection of His Mother means rejection of Him. Jesus is Mary, Mary is Jesus. Moreover, to reach the Eternal Father one goes through Jesus but to reach Jesus in order to reached the Eternal Father is through Mary.

> O Mary my Mother, Queen of my heart,
> purify my heart, adorn my soul with your

Virtues, make me more attractive for Jesus Your Son, my most Charming, Wonderful, Beautiful Bridegroom to induce Him always to have delight in my company and desire me much more than I do Him. I love You Mum.

When everyone abandoned Her Son she stood by Him, suffered bitterly with Him in Her heart. She bore with Him all the humiliation, scourging, agony, crowning with thorns, lacerations, mockery in all its details, the crucifixion and the awful abandonment of God the Father. All that Her Divine Son Jesus Christ experienced in His Blessed Body, physically and mentally She experienced in Her Heart, as She sacrificed Her one and only Son, Her only Love, Her Spouse and Her God in obedience to the Eternal Father for the salvation of humanity. Humanity will never know all Jesus had to tolerate, the terrible depth of His pains nor the depth of sorrow in the Immaculate Heart of His Blessed Mother. Had God not sustained Her, for Her motherly role in the new Israel, the Church, the sorrow in Her Heart would have killed Her. She is the model of every Christian, perfect in obedience to the Word of God, embedded with the Virtues of God, Love and Mercy.

Our Lord Jesus Christ is delighted when His Mother is honored. To honor His Mother is to honor Him. Therefore, to easily reach Jesus is to approach Him through the Immaculate Heart of His Holy Mother. To reject the Holy Mother of God is an insult to the Lord Jesus Christ, a rejection of His Person, a denial of His Humanity, an underestimation of His Virtues, His Divine nature Love, His infinite Goodness and Mercy. Mary belongs to God's plan to defeat Satan, the powers of darkness, which He has already done with the triumph of His Holy Cross and His glorious resurrection. She belongs to His Vision for humanity, His Children to whom He gave His Heart, loves with a motherly love, God's Family, the new Israel of the new covenant.

If God in His infinite Wisdom had wanted any other of His Apostles to be the one to stand at the foot of the cross with His Beloved Mother He would have made it possible. The choice of the Beloved Apostle, John, to whom He entrusted His Mother is significant as it portrayed His deep love for the Church He was founding on Peter, for the members of His mystical Body. Therefore, failure to accept and love His Mother is going against God's Divine plan. Should there be any obstacle to loving Mary Jesus will help if His Help is genuinely sought. Some people, however, misinterpret "Son behold your mother" for their own purpose, choosing the broad way for their comfort, consequently falling into the trap of the enemy and in their own conceit go against the Holy Will of God.

Besides, one must not forget that no one heard and obeyed the Word of God as the Blessed Virgin Mary. Though conceived without sin and full of Grace She retained Her free-will. God Who is Love, does not force one to love Him. It must be an act of free-will to give one's heart to God to receive God's Love. Her "Yes" to God portrays Her humility, trust and total submission of self to God's Love for Her, thereby making the Incarnation possible which led to the ultimate salvation of humanity. At the greeting of the Angel to Mary "Hail, full of grace, the Lord is with you!" Mary's humble reply to the message of St. Gabriel, the Archangel, after she knew the reason for the beautiful greeting was "How can this be, since I have no husband?" And the Angel assured her saying "The Holy Spirit will come upon you, and the power of the Most High will overshadow you: therefore the child to be born will be called Holy, the Son of God. And behold, your kinswoman Elizabeth in her old age has also conceived a son; and this is the sixth month with her who was called barren. For with God nothing will be impossible" And then came Mary's humble reply that gave relief to the Heart of God and paved way to the realization of His Vision for humanity who have stolen His Heart as His Beloved Children, "Behold, I am the handmaid of the Lord; let it be to me according to your word" Thereafter, Mary conceived and became the Mother of God, Mother of the Word Incarnate, who in turn gave her, His Mother, to Humanity as their Mother. She is to be accepted and recognized as such, loved and honored, this being God's Holy Will, in order to belong to the Family of God here on earth, in His Church, that will be perfected in Heaven. She is the Mother of all God's children, of all humanity.

Mary, whose womb was the first Tabernacle of the Holy Trinity – God, said all generations will call her blessed, in response to the greeting of Elizabeth, the mother of John the Baptist, who being filled with the Holy Spirit, leaped in his mother's womb with joy at the presence of the Holy Trinity in the womb of Mary. ' In those days Mary arose and went with haste into the hill country, to a city of Judah, and she greeted Elizabeth. And when Elizabeth heard the greeting of Mary, the babe leaped in her womb, and Elizabeth was filled with the Holy spirit and she exclaimed with a loud cry', "Blessed are you among women and blessed is the fruit of your womb! And why is this granted me that the mother of my Lord should come to me? For behold, when the voice of your greeting came to my ears, the babe in my womb leaped for joy. And blessed is she who believed that there would be a fulfilment of what was spoken to her from the Lord" Mary responded "My soul magnifies the Lord, and my spirit rejoices in God my Savior, for he has regarded the low estate of his handmaiden. For behold henceforth all generations will call me blessed; for he who is mighty has done great things for me, and holy is his name. And his mercy is on those who fear him from generation to generation. He has shown strength with his arm, he has scattered the proud in the imagination of their hearts, he has put down the mighty from their thrones, and exalted those of low degree; he has filled the hungry with good things, and the rich he has sent empty away. He has helped his servant Israel, in remembrance of his mercy, as he spoke to our fathers, to Abraham and to his posterity forever"

It should be emphasized Jesus said "If you have seen me you have seen the Father" "I and the Father are one", therefore, Mary is the Mother of God, afterall this is what Elizabeth, under the influence of the Holy Spirit, called Her. However, if God Himself revealed through Elizabeth that Mary is His Mother who is man that he should doubt? Where Jesus is, the Father and the Holy Spirit also are. The Father and the Holy Spirit are in Jesus. Jesus is God. God is a triune God, the indivisible Trinity. This is the mystery of God which Jesus our Lord Himself revealed therefore, so it is, so it has to be accepted.

"And blessed is she who believed that there would be a fulfilment of what was spoken to her from the Lord" An excellent testimony of the Holy Spirit, about Mary, through Elizabeth for hearing and responding to the Word of God. Jesus did not intimidate Mary as some protestant Christians believe, when He said "My mother and my brethren are those who hear the word of God and do it" Is there anyone who heard and did the word of God better than Mary who, though She did not understand, trusted in God's love for Her. Jesus is the one and only Son of Mary. Her involvement in the Divine Plan, did not leave room for another child, after Jesus, as this would have been a hindrance to Her perfect role as the Mother of humanity. Nobody, except Jesus, should have a special claim to Her. God is not partial. She is Mother to everyone, Her love is for everyone. It did not matter if you rejected Her She loves you. However, failure to accept Her means rejecting Jesus, rejecting God's Love and His Vision. Jesus is Love and Mary is Love. God fashioned and enriched Her with His Virtues therefore, God's Love and Mary's Love remain for you despite your rejecting them, but you may not be able to fathom the pain your rejection cause them. You are their Child! Love never fails but you will have no share with them if you rejected them with your free-will.

However, should you feel you have come short of God's Love, rather than grumbling, a thorough examination of conscience, self-criticism, would do no harm, perhaps you may discover the fault is not in your star but in you, maybe you are wanting in keeping God's Precepts and in prayer. Moreover, rejection of Mary as Mother is to deny oneself the luxury of the loving tender care of a sweet loving Mother, and so reject God's plan, and forfeit a share in the Beatific vision of our Lord Jesus Christ in Heaven.

I swim in admiration for the Almighty Father whose fatherly love is so overwhelming. Jesus is the best Father. It is astonishing though, some people do not share this admiration, therefore, rather than express love to the Almighty Father, in Jesus Christ, using the Blessed Virgin Mary as their model, they prefer to give that love to a public figure, for example, a musician, an actress or an actor. In some cases, even a politician, their so called ideal, who is unaware of their existence. They emulate their mode of life, which in most cases is worldly and leads undoubtedly, to perdition if they failed to return to the Almighty Father in humble trust before the expiration of life. Whereas if Jesus, the only begotten Son of the Father, Lord of Heaven and Earth, Author and Giver of life, Who is madly in love with humanity, is chosen, as Ideal, His mode of life emulated, one is undoubtedly guaranteed Eternal life in eternity. Attention should be paid to the Father's unceasing caution of danger, His attempt for all to be aware of the inevitable perdition in allowing oneself to be trapped by Satan with the transitory riches of this world that would be destroyed by fire. Whenever His Children are faced with a challenge God always provides them the means to face the challenge. O what a wonderful Father!

The Church has so many Saints, people like you and me, who surrendered their lives to God's Holy Will, emulated Jesus as their Ideal and made Heaven, whose lives are a help for us to shape our respective life to the delight of God. In these days of secularism and media ideology God gave us a television sender, The Eternal Word Television Network for the propagation of the Catholic Faith. At the fullness of time the Lord Jesus chose His humble Nun, mother Angelica, who gave her "Yes" to Him for this purpose without counting the cost, trusting in God's Love and in His Faithfulness. This way she was able to start a satellite television network with nothing. The Almighty God provided the means for it. Everything and everyone belong to God. He uses what belongs to Him to work out His purposes whenever He chooses. This Television Network is an asset to the Catholic Church in defending and propagating the Catholic Faith to the world. It is a treasure for Catholics who are bedridden and cannot attend Mass and for those who deviated from their Faith due to lack of knowledge of the Treasure of their Catholic Faith and also for none Catholics to learn and understand what Catholics believe to hasten their return to their roots. It is indispensable for none Catholic Christians whose interest lies in being in compliance with the Holy Will of God, who desire to find out the very Church Jesus founded and gave His word "gate of hell will not prevail against Her" When Jesus, who is God, says His One, Holy, Catholic and Apostolic Church will remain till the end of time, She will. The Church has gone through many waters from the moment of Her founding, yet She still exists, over 2000 years, two Millennium, she has been on Her pilgrim journey, so must She in this 3rd Millennium according to God's Holy Will, because God said so, until Jesus returns to judge the living and the dead. The second coming of Jesus is for judgement, now is the moment of Divine Mercy.

As it pleased God I had the Grace to experience the most beautiful phenomenon of our Catholic Faith, how wonderful, on EWTN – Eternal Word Television Network. To watch the afternoon Mass is a usual habit of mine, therefore, on this day 30th August 2013, after the Mass, the prayer of St. Michael the Archangel was said, but as I was adoring the Lord in the Monstrance, as usual, which is usually exposed after the prayer of St Michael, suddenly, like in a trance, instead of the Monstrance I saw the Host in an empty Church moving backwards, as though it was being zoomed backwards. Inside the Host was the Blessed Virgin, our Lady holding the Baby Jesus in Her Arms with such loving tenderness that portrayed a mother deeply in love with Her Baby. The Blessed Virgin held Her Baby affectionately, elevating His head towards

Herself while bending forward, looking into His eyes as though she would kiss Him. I was swept in awe of admiration deeply moved by such loving expression and the depth of love between our Lord and His Mother. In the same fashion does our Lady love each one of us, Her children if we accept Her and welcome Her in our lives. It all depends on our free-will just as it depends on our free-will to accept God's Love or reject it. The Lord has granted me many graces from watching EWTN. In the same way, during the Divine Mercy prayer in sung, while contemplating on the Lords passion, His Arm on one of the crosses, with numerous wounds on His Body, became alive. Ever since then each time I say the Divine Mercy in sung with EWTN the Arm becomes alive, the fingers outstretched and gradually folded back into position. If I failed to look up at once the Lord waits for me. It is awesome. God is wonderful and most merciful. The graces He grants me I do not deserve as I am most unworthy, a nobody, less than half of an Ant, yet, I am very grateful to God for loving someone like me, for tolerating me. I pray to be worthy of His Love for me.

It is good to know that when Jesus is received in the Eucharist His Mother is also there. Jesus and Mary are inseparable, hence Her Blood flows in His veins. Mary is the Mother of the Eucharist, the Eucharist is Jesus, besides from Mary Jesus took His human Body. A beautiful Mystery. Jesus, the Eucharistic Lord, Mary, the Mother and Queen of the Eucharist. We are the Children of the Eucharist. In the consecrated Host is the Godhead, the Holy Trinity, therefore, we do not receive Jesus only but the Holy Trinity. What a wonderful beautiful Grace of God to humanity, the Beauty of the Father's Love! What a privilege to be Catholic! Jesus does not live in a soul alone but with His Father and the Holy Spirit. I am so grateful to God for Mum's love. She is the perfect Mum and I love Her so must you for Her "Yes" paved way for us to belong to the Family of God, to become the children of the indivisible Trinity, sons and daughters of the Almighty God, the great I AM, What a blessing to humanity!

"Everyone who believes that Jesus is the Christ is a child of God, and every one who loves the parent loves the child" 1 Jn 5 vs 1 For those who want to see where it is in the bible, this is it. To believe Jesus is the Christ makes one a child of God, but one must believe in the parent of the child. The parent of the child is Mary His Mother. It is clear She is the one referred to here. Jesus in his humanity is the child whose parent is Mary. There is nowhere God is referred to in the bible as parent, but "Father" therefore one who truly loves Jesus loves His Mother and only through His Mother Jesus can be reached so as to reach the Father through Him. When you love His Mother, then you are His brother, His sister.

CHAPTER XII

THE PRIEST

"Not all men can receive this precept, but only those to whom it is given. For there are eunuchs who have been so from birth, and there are eunuchs who have been made eunuchs by men, and there are eunuchs who have made themselves eunuchs for the sake of the kingdom of heaven. He who is able to receive this, let him receive it" Matt. 19 vs. 11-12. Celibacy is a gift of God and a tremendous blessing which should not be taken lightly. Priesthood is a key to the Sacred Heart of Jesus Which is the easiest way to Heaven, Jesus is Heaven. A passionate priest is constantly in God's love. Jesus cautions to abide in His Love, that's exactly what the priest does every day of His life as long as he keeps his focus on Jesus. Jesus loves His priest. He needs him for His Eucharistic Presence. It is an honor, a privilege to be a priest, not to be abused.

A priest should aspire to be "the faithful and wise servant whom his master has set over his household, to give them their food at the proper time" and not the wicked servant who says to himself "My master is delayed; and begins to beat his fellow servants, and eats and drinks with the drunken, the master of that servant will come on a day when he does not expect him and at an hour he does not know, and will punish him, and put him with the hypocrites, there men will weep and gnash their teeth." Matt. 24 vs. 45 – 51 Such would be the fate of some priests who abuse the priesthood in different ways that dishonor the Body of Christ, the Church. What a tragedy for the souls of such priests!

It is quite natural, to show sympathy to someone close, someone dear, yes, to the needy and even to criminals, considering the poor state of their souls. That is quite alright, such is pleasing to God but should God Himself come short of our attention and sympathy in the course of it? How dishearteningly disappointing the Almighty Father is often denied sympathy in the course of it all. Perhaps, one might ask, how can the Almighty God, Creator of all that is, seen and unseen, Lord of Heaven and Earth, Author and Giver of Life, the Supreme Majesty, the great I AM be pitied when He is Lord of Creation and everything belongs to Him? This is the thought of so many of God's children, including some of those who believe in Him yet do not understand Love. Failure to understand the infinite Love in God's Heart for humanity instigates such people to believe in their heart they themselves are the ones who need to be pitied, feeling God does not care about them, therefore they begin to seek relief from their poor social status outside of God, overburdened with their misery. In fact to such an extent they become resistant to reason, encaged in their little world, prisoners of their misconception, unwilling to make proper use of their intellect.

Under this self-imposed condition they fail to realize their sorry state in falling short of their responsibility to their Creator and Father by denying Him their love, which consequently makes them unable to realize that God, their Father, is unhappy over His unrequited love. If anyone deserves sympathy, it is the Almighty Father Who has been robbed the right to enjoy His Creation in which He was delighted, the joy of Fatherhood. That a created being, Satan, the wicked devil, dared oppose God, denied obeisance to the second Person of the Trinity, tempted and deceived Eve who in turn implicated her husband Adam, which led to their consequent removal from the garden of Eden where they lacked nothing, is an unforgivable crime. In his arrogance, Satan reduced himself to a replica of death, ugly and smelly. Having segregated with a third of the angels and driven away from Heaven he wanted to possess the Earth which he did not create, with his fellow wicked spirits, to hurt the Almighty Father by tampering with humanity whom God created for Himself in His own image, endowed with all His Love and regards them as His beloved Children. The devil's insatiability for wickedness, on which he exists, is the motive which instigates him to poison the minds of humanity by feeding their minds with fallacious fallacy, his deceitful means of presenting them with the wrong image of God to turn them against Him, their own Father, who loves them infinitely. Awake, o man, be aware of the feelings of your God, of your Father. "Resist the devil and he will flee from you."

On 04.10.13, the feast of the Sacred Heart of our Lord, walking happily to Mass through my usual route, a cemented pathway, knowing fully well Jesus was going with me and would bring me safely home, confidently, as I walked, I began contemplating on my resolution to suffer with Him. Surprisingly as I began to do so, suddenly, Satan pushed me and I fell down. On seeing the pavement on which I was to hit my head I felt a certain dizziness and shouted immediately "My Lord Jesus" before falling down supporting myself on my palms. Fortunately, due to the grace of God, I was saved from hitting my head on the pavement which would have been very fatal. It would have landing me in a hospital. I would have missed the Mass and the Eucharist which I love. Satan's plan was to deprive me from receiving Jesus in the Eucharist without whom I cannot exist. I love Jesus in the Eucharist. He is my life. However, thankfully I got up rejoicing for the grace to suffer for the love of Jesus to the disappointment of Satan who expected me to blame God for not preventing me from falling down having relied on Him to see me safely to Mass and bring me safely home. Whenever Satan plays his tricks without success he becomes uneasy. Therefore, the sympathy for our Heavenly Father, accepting whatever suffering one may encounter with love, without grumbling, confidently aware no hair of ours would fall without the consent of our Heavenly Father, would always keep the enemy uneasy. With this on mind every priest should pray to bear all things for the love of God, live what he preaches and be able to say "for me to live is Christ and to die is gain" The priest is another Christ, therefore live as Christ lived.

"I am the Vine and you are the branches" Jesus said, therefore, we are all members of His Mystical Body the church. But one thing is sure, the priest has a special position in the Church, hence he is the beauty of the Church, the garland with which the Church is ornamented. A priest plays a significant role in the mystical Body of Christ, specially blessed by God and greatly treasured in the most Sacred Heart of Jesus. Jesus is the Key to Heaven and He is Heaven. The priest possesses this Key to Heaven, himself being another Christ. If only the priest knew how treasured he is in the Most Sacred Heart of Jesus He would do everything possible to cherish and appreciate his priesthood. He would keep his focus always on Jesus and renew regularly his priestly vows so as not to give the crafty enemy, Satan, any room to dare to divert his focus away from His Divine Master. It does not suffice to be a mere priest, but rather a passionate priest whose sole intent is to give his all for the service of the crucified One, His Lord and Master, who sacrificed His Life for love of him. Jesus is God and God is the same yesterday, today and tomorrow.

Although we have a Humble and merciful God, He deserves reverence which should be portrayed to the laity in the way and manner the priest carries himself in general as servant of a Holy God and more so at the Altar while he conducts Mass and especially during the Liturgy of the Eucharist when He acts in Persona Christi. The serenity of God's holiness exhibited by the priest, especially at the Altar, imparts a feeling of awe on the Laity, awakening in them the awareness of the Supremacy, Divinity and Majesty of the all-powerful God who created them with such infinite Love. For the Laity, the priest is the authority and example to be emulated as a representative of Jesus Christ. The priest is to reflect the beauty of God, His awesomeness and His Supreme Majesty. In doing so the Laity would begin to absorb and to be aware of the need to abide in the Love of the God who created them and adorned them with His infinite Love and so aim at keeping His commandment with love and awe. This would also enable them keep their focus in Heaven and not relax depending only on God's Mercy, which of course is infinite, but just as faith without work is dead so is relaxation without genuine work of Mercy and repentance short of Divine Mercy. The early Church fathers knew well enough to give reverence to the Lord of Heaven and Earth, an example which should be indispensable to Christians in the same way as Air, food and water are indispensable to life for God does not change. Souls with genuine love for God knows to reverence God, they delight Him.

A priest is dignified in his priestly habit, but when he chooses to dress himself in plain clothes like the common people he degrades himself and tarnishes his image as a priest. In declining to wear his priestly habit he exposes himself to temptation and becomes more or less an easy target for Satan who is working round the clock to reach him. The priestly habit is a constant reminder to the priest of who he is and Who he serves. If one is aware he is surrounded by enemies, the wisest thing to do is to be watchful and not to pave way for his enemies to reach him. Besides, it is the Divine Will a priest should wear religious Habit as a sign of his office in reverence to God. Religious Habits and Vestments are pleasing to the Lord when his priests wear them, or are those priests who move about in plain clothes ashamed of their priestly vocation? One must not forget the Lord will also be ashamed of anyone who is ashamed of Him before His Father. Do you not realize the priestly habit is prestigious? One must not use the Vatican Council II as a camouflage for unfaithfulness to the Lord Jesus Christ for God cannot be deceived.

In the Mosaic time when Aaron was ordained a priest the Lord ordered a garment should be made for him. "The holy garment of Aaron shall be for his sons after him, to be anointed in them and ordained in them. The son who is priest in his place shall wear them seven days, when he comes into the tent of meeting to minister in the holy place" Ex. 29 vs 29. "And of the blue and purple and scarlet stuff they made finely wrought garments, for ministering in the holy place; they made the holy garments for Aaron, as the Lord had commanded Moses. And he made ephod of gold, blue and purple and scarlet stuff, and fine twined linen. And gold leaf was hammered out and cut into threads to work into the blue and purple and the scarlet stuff, and into the fine twined linen, in skilled design. They made for the ephod shoulder-pieces, joined to it at its two edges. And the skillfully woven band upon it. to gird it on, was of the same materials and workmanship, of gold, blue and purple and scarlet stuff, and fine twined linen; as the Lord had commanded Moses" Ex.39 vs. 1 – 5. A priest should not be ashamed to wear his habit which is an independent witness of his Faith. The priestly habit speaks for itself. It witnesses for Christ. A true and honest lover does not hide his love rather he shows his love proudly to the whole world. The priestly habit portrays respect and awe for God and at the same time acts as a constant reminder to the priest of who he actually is and grants him constant awareness of his Divine Master. In fact any priest who has a genuine love for Jesus would not hesitate to wear his priestly habit as this is pleasing to Him who loves him so infinitely and elevated him highly in His Most Sacred Heart. Do not allow the misinterpretation of the second Vatican Council be an impediment to your faithfulness to the God of Love. Jesus is the Supreme authority, the Supreme Majesty, nothing else matters but Him and His Holy Will is priority and final.

"Who then is the faithful and wise servant, whom his master has set over his household, to give them their food at the proper time? Blessed is that servant whom his master when he comes will find so doing. Truly, I say to you, he will set him over all his possessions. But if that wicked servant says to himself, 'My master is delayed,' and begins to beat his fellow servants, and eats and drinks with the drunken, the master will come on a day when he does not expect him and at an hour he does not know, and will punish him, and put him with the hypocrites; there men will weep and gnash their teeth." Matt. 24 vs. 45 ".

Despite the generosity of the Lord to priests adorning them with a special grace and granting them a special place in His Most Sacred Heart, yet, some priests misuse this favor ruthlessly without a thought for the Good Lord they hurt. To acquire worldly possession even at the risk of perdition they leave their Lord and Master in continuous agony. It is sad to observe this plague also in some Bishops who are in the lineage of the apostles who should know better, but are rather instrumental for the enemy of God who is constantly challenging the Highest God, the Almighty Father who loves humanity with infinite Love desiring everyone to be saved, hurting the Most Sacred Heart of Jesus who bled to give us life. What does it profit such priests, Bishops to dwell in sin that grace may abound? Why sin willfully to receive the Sacrament of reconciliation thereafter? Why try God? The riches of this world passes away. Hell is also for Priests, Bishops and everyone in defiance of the Law of God.

Has Jesus not been humiliated enough, has He not suffered enough for humanity? If the world does not understand at least His priests should. Why should those least expected to disgrace Him be the ones to do so. Those meant to live exemplary life are those who indulge in moral decay leading innocent children to sin. This is simply an abuse of office crucifying their Master all over again with their sinfulness. Such priests and bishops have no excuse to crucify the Lord a second time, staining the priesthood and the Bishop staff. Of course, not all priests and bishops indulge in such evil practices. There are a large number of dedicated, passionate priests and bishops faithful to their crucified Lord who realize His Blood leaves their lips purpled at every Eucharistic Mass. Bearing on mind priests and bishops are not exempted from perdition, if they failed to live up to expectation, they should be always aware of the crafty enemy, the devil, who prowls around the world for the ruin of souls. They should not forget they are the devils target and as such should always be alert, keeping their focus on Jesus who is able to sustain and shield them from our salvation's enemy. Jesus never lost His focus on His mission, always in constant contact with His Father in prayer, so He was able to fulfill the Father's Will even unto death, therefore, as shepherds of His flock, keeping focus on Him and emulating Him is the wisest thing to do.

"Whoever causes one of these little ones who believe in me to sin, it would be better for him if a great millstone were hung round his neck and he were thrown into the sea. And if your hand causes you to sin, cut it off; it is better for you to enter life maimed than with two hands to go to hell, to the unquenchable fire. And if your foot causes you to sin, cut it off; it is better for you to enter life lame than with two feet to be thrown into hell. And if your eye causes you to sin, pluck it out; it is better for you to enter the kingdom of God with one eye than with two eyes to be thrown into hell, where their worm does not die, and the fire is not quenched" Mk 9 vs 42 – 48

There are, unfortunately, some priests and Bishops who offend their Divine Master with the hope to end up in Purgatory, after all Heaven is the ultimate destination for those in Purgatory they presume. Yes, but how wrong they are! They may be disappointed to find themselves in Hell and not in Purgatory. It must not be forgotten that our good Lord is a just God, rendering to everyone his due reward. Of course, as already mentioned, the priest has a special place in the Most Sacred Heart of Jesus, so does the bishop but they have to prove themselves worthy of it. How could a priest or bishop, for instance, cause some little ones who believe in our Lord Jesus Christ to sin and hope to end up in Heaven. It would take a deep and honest repentance for such a priest or bishop to receive God's Mercy whose Heart of Love they wound without consideration of the agony they constantly inflict on His Most Sacred Heart, on their Divine Master who has generously elevated them. Having come to the true knowledge of the truth, to fall woefully and willfully into mortal sin is indeed a dreadful and pitiable failure. Anyone called to the priesthood by Divine incentive should appreciate the call with enthusiasm, considering himself favored to be chosen, having every resolution to prove himself worthy of the Divine honor, relying on Divine assistance, staying with our Lady at the foot of the cross, refilling ones energy from the Blessed Sacrament in daily adoration and prayer so as to be immune to the temptations of the enemy of the Holy Cross of Salvation. Do not trouble the Lord who has done so much for humanity any more. Be master of your will with the Master's Help, return fully to Him who loves you infinitely and serve Him well for your happiness. His Divine Mercy should not be taken for granted, one must aim to be worthy of it.

CHAPTER XIII

AWARENESS

O my people, my people, how long do you want to leave me bleeding and in agony for love of you. What have I not done for you O you of little faith. How long do you still want to punish this Heart that has loved so much. Why do you burden your hearts with iniquity, with the sinful pleasures of this terrible world. They are sins from hell which Satan uses to destroy the Temple of the Holy Spirit which is your body. Have pity on your God who is running helter-skelter for your salvation. All you seek and run after you have in abundance in me. Open up your heart, surrender yourself to me. I am your Love, I am a God of Love, I am Love. I created you with Love, you are made for Love. Live your life in me and for me and you will possess all you seek. Only in me you have life and peace, carry your crosses and follow me, there is no other way my children except the way of the cross. Remember, I have gone this way and my mother too. Whatever suffering you encounter offer it to me in atonement for your sins and those of the whole world. I am always there, your Jesus, to help you, do not be disheartened, do not despair, simply trust in me and draw strength from my Holy Cross. My Sacred Heart and the Immaculate Heart of my Mother will triumph. The two Hearts of Love will triumph, be not afraid.

Why are my Bishops and Priests disgracing me. Have I not been disgraced enough already? Why do some of them act like the Pharisees and Scribes of today, hypocrites! who appear like whitewashed tombs, outwardly they appear beautiful but inside they are full of dead men's bones and all uncleanness. Outwardly they appear righteous to men, but within they are full of hypocrisy and iniquity leading little ones who love me to sin. They run after worldly goods even at the risk of perdition. Yes, I am a God of Love and Mercy but also a righteous Judge. Any branch which does not produce good fruit will be hewed down. Whoever rejects my Mercy will meet my judgement. My Bishops, the successors of my apostles who should know better to protect my interest in this terrifying wilderness are those who hurt me most. Have I not been humiliated enough? Why do they join unbelievers to persecute me. Let my Bishops and Priests return to me, return to your Master and Savior who is in agony.

Jesus is pleading to you to return to Him. Show pity and concern for your crucified Lord. Be aware of who you are and whom you serve. Do you not realize the suffering of our Lord Jesus Christ o you Bishops and Priests who disgrace Him? Do you not realize, you who are consecrated to Him hurt Him the most? What is there in the worldly riches and pleasure that is so enticing as to keep you from being aware you are treading on dangerous ground? Failure to be conscious of the malicious enemy of humanity from whom the good Lord, bought us free with a bitter price, the shedding of His Most Precious Blood spells danger eternally. Jesus tries to protect you, but you would not let Him merely for the pleasures and riches of this transitory world that lead to perdition. If these things you seek are transitory and would be destroyed by fire why run after them when they lead to perdition, why hurt your Master? Do you not realize your indulgence in sin, oblivious of the malicious enemy leaves one wondering at the sincerity of your love for Him whom you profess to love and serve? His Supreme Majesty, the Almighty God, to whom everything belongs, took flesh, was born poor, lived poor, died poor, even His tomb did not belong to Him. He owns everything and yet he had nothing during His earthly life. Do you not realize the significance of it? Treasures are to be stored in Heaven not in a world that has no future. You are not unaware of this truth. Do not sin, with the notion, after I will go to confession, God cannot be deceived. Bad nuts should not soil good ones, they should be sieved. Why are you in such a hurry to receive reward for your labor in this world which will be extinguished by fire? Don't you realize a patient dog eats the fattest bone and that patience is the crown of fidelity? The reward of a faithful servant of the Divine Master is Eternal life in Heaven. One cannot eat his cake and have it. To cause the Lord agony having come to the full knowledge of the truth is an atrocity, yet our merciful Lord forgives if genuine repentance is made with the intention not to fall back willfully to sin.

".... for whatever overcomes a man, to that he is enslaved. For if, after they have escaped the defilements of the world through the knowledge of our Lord and Savior Jesus Christ, they are again entangled in them and overpowered, the last state has become worse for them than the first. For it would have been better for them never to have known the way of righteousness than after knowing it to turn back from the holy commandment delivered to them. It has happened to them according to the true proverb, the dog turns back to his own vomit, and the sow is washed only to wallow in the mire" 2 peter 2 vs 19 – 22

It does not pay to sin, with the intention afterwards to receive the Sacrament of Reconciliation. It is unwise to take the Lords Mercy for granted. The Sacrament of Reconciliation is not for a particular set of the clergy and laity but for every member of the Mystical Body of Christ. Everyone should receive this Sacrament regularly, including the Bishops and the Priests, in order to receive grace from God to avoid any bad conduct. Frequent reception of this Sacrament is humbling and keeps one always in a state of Grace for the reception of the Holy Eucharist. Jesus would not have instituted the Sacraments if there was no need for them. After all, He said we cannot do anything without Him and asked that we should abide in His Love, by observing His commandments. To enable us do so He instituted the Sacraments from which we receive sanctifying Grace. If St. John Paul II who lived an exemplary life, who was regarded as a Saint in his life time, received the Sacrament of Reconciliation every week or two, what stops the Bishops and Priests, who dishonor Jesus, from frequent visit to the confessional, at least once a month, unless they have lost confidence in their Divine Master, like the servant who felt his master delayed in returning and began to punish his fellow servants, squandering his masters goods until his masters return took him unaware. Jesus is in agony due to the coldness, lack of trust and indifference by which we respond to His Love. All the Bishops and Priests who prefer the riches and pleasures of this world rather than wait for your reward in Heaven, if that is your choice, then be at least polite, step down to pursue your interest but stop staining the priesthood and the Bishops staff. Let faithful priests and Bishops regain their image, as servants of their Divine Master who serve Him in holiness and in truth. Do not forget, the Lord is able to make stones rise up to become Priests and Bishops to serve Him. The Church lives, Jesus lives, gate of hell will never prevail against His Church, it didn't matter which course you choose Jesus is Lord, He has spoken and so it will be.

How awesome, this wonderful truth, the Highest God, Jesus Christ is present in the Tabernacle in every Catholic Church, a lonely Prisoner of love for you and me. This is hard to believe, but it is true. Jesus the Savior of the world has made this prison His Home on Earth in His Church, the One, Holy, Catholic and Apostolic Church. His Sanctuary in which the Divine Presence of the Holy Trinity is filled. It is a beautiful Truth that deserves admiration and wonder at the Infinite Power of the Almighty God of all Creation to reduce Himself into bread, His Beauty hidden in the Host for humanity. Jesus promised not to leave us as orphans, as a faithful God whose word never returns to Him empty kept His promise, this way, with His Divine Presence in the Tabernacle. What a marvelous Truth, far beyond human comprehension, how the Almighty God, Author and Giver of Life, the great I AM, chooses to be in prison and in such a prison. One is left with awesome admiration at the humility of God. If He could create the Universe and the Firmament and if He could take Flesh in the womb of a Virgin, undoubtedly He is in the lonely Tabernacle because He said He is. Besides, as a loving Father who craves for the love of His Children, whose fatherly protective instinct leaves Him with no other option, than keep sacrificing Himself in love in order to secure for humanity the glory that was theirs from the foundation of the world He has to do what He must do. This God who created humanity, gave His Love to humanity, calls Himself the Father of humanity, loves humanity with a mother's love, will stop at nothing for the happiness and salvation of humanity. Love is the cause of the suffering of our good Lord. His nature is love. He cannot be otherwise. This love keeps Him prisoner in the Tabernacles of the world. Unfortunately, His Divine Presence is scarcely noticed, nor reverenced accordingly. The unrequited love breaks His Most Sacred Heart. Inside the Tabernacle Jesus observes, with God the Father and the Holy Spirit, who live in Him, the indifferences, disrespect, lack of reverence, sacrileges, lack of awe by which the Almighty God is approached. The nonchalant attitude by which He is received in the Sacrament of His Love breaks His Heart. O how often do I weep with my God for the coldness of humanity to His beautiful Love brought home to us through the Incarnation of the Word, our Savior Jesus Christ. Such beautiful Love of our Lord and Master deserves reciprocation with grateful affection in humble trust.

> O Sacred Heart of Jesus Christ, my sweet Beloved,
> Burning Furnace of Love, abode of the Holy Trinity,
> Abyss of suffering, consume me with your Love that
> I be love as You, united with You in suffering. I am
> Your Victim of Love O sweet suffering of Love Divine.
>
> A Host I do desire to be, my sweet lonely Prisoner in
> the Tabernacle, that I may gladly join You, O my sweet
> Beloved Divine, in loving tenderness, Your loneliness
> to share, so as to fill the Tabernacle with the sweetness
> and fragrance of Love in complete surrender of self.

O Sweet Heart of Love, my sweet Beloved dear, a Host, Yes, O sweet Host I do desire to be, in loving union with You my Beloved, You who my heart has stolen to be tightly enclosed in Your Most Sacred Heart, my sweet Refuge, always by You in all the Tabernacles of the world.

Your sweet victim of Love I be to use and do as it pleases You. In humbleness of heart, deeply pierced with Your arrows of Love, completely united in Your Suffering, pain, agony, and sorrows, crowned in union with You O Divine Love of mine in perfect Bliss.

It is most astonishing the attack of the circular media on the Holy Church of God, the instrument which the devil uses against the Holy cross of salvation. This calls for total vigilance and caution on the part of the Bishops and the Clergy, as they are open letters and continuous targets of the enemy of the Church. It is therefore expected of them to always put on the amour of God, fully prepared to face the coward enemy, Satan, who already defeated, is bent on taking as many souls as possible with him to perdition. They should prove themselves equal to the task of guarding and nourishing the faithful with sound doctrine according to our Catholic Faith by keeping their focus on Jesus, their Divine Master. Oblivion is a disease that should not be found among the Clergy and the Bishops to avoid distraction and deviation from the task of tending the sheep entrusted to their care by Jesus, and become 'easy stuff' for the media, the instrument of Satan to tarnish the image of the Church. The circular media should not be given room to be mouthy, as a result of unfaithfulness to Jesus, their Spouse, with the abuse of innocent children He entrusted to their care. It would be unwise, premature thought and unreasonable to under estimate the Lord Jesus, who is the Pilot of His Ship, the Church, like the Ark of Noah, for He will surely bring His Ship to safety. He is God, a most good God who says and it is, most faithful and most trustworthy. His silence and Divine Mercy should not be taken for granted. It is not granted to anyone to tarnish the image of the priesthood.

Rather than provide room for temptations, Bishops should pay more attention to what goes on in their respective Dioceses, making sure the Faithful are fed with the true doctrine of our Catholic Faith, especially children, during catechism. Many parishes do not even have adoration hours any more, except for first Friday in the month, sometimes this is neglected. The faithful desire to spend time with their Lord and Master, with Jesus. It is most unfortunate most priests are no longer able to meet up with this demand due to the scarcity of priests. In Germany for instance, where priests seem to be more scarce, it is difficult to find a parish with daily adoration. As strength and direction of the members of the Mystical Body of Christ are drawn from the Sacraments and from adoration of the Blessed Sacrament, there is need to create room for adoration even if priests are scarce. It is true prayers are made for priestly vocations and for consecrated life, yet it should not be forgotten that faith without work is dead, therefore adoration is essential. Adoration is also essential not only for vocations but also for the fulfillment in living the Catholic life. Regular adoration of the Blessed Sacrament makes every burden lighter, directions, with regards to vocations, become clearer, love for God increases, one becomes more equipped, with the Grace of God, to resist the devil, ailments are avoided, should there be any there would be strength to bear it for the love of God.

The reason some priests do not encourage adoration is due to their full calendar. They would rather make time for their recreation than adoration time for the faithful who hunger to adore their Lord Jesus Christ. Every Catholic is called to be a saint therefore, it would be beneficial for them as well if they offered their inconvenience to Jesus. Adoration refreshes, it is a source of refilling the energy spent just as the filling station is a place for cars to refill their tanks with petrol or gas to keep moving. Adoration is essential, it is not enough to refer the faithful to the Tabernacle, when they can have the Good Lord brought out to be admired and adored, looking at Him while He looks back at them. Besides, Jesus who has been a prisoner of Love in the Tabernacle for over two thousand years, will appreciate it if brought out for at least an hour, to be beheld by His beloved Children while He beholds them as they adore Him. He finds delight in this as Father.

"O God, thou art my God, I seek thee, my soul thirst for thee; my flesh faints for thee, as in a dry and weary land where no water is. So I have looked upon thee in the sanctuary, beholding thy power and glory. Because thy steadfast love is better than life, my lips will praise thee. So I will bless thee as long as I live; I will lift up my hands and call on thy name. My soul is feasted as with marrow and fat, and my mouth praises thee with joyful lips, when I think of thee upon my bed, and meditate on thee in the watches of the night; for thou hast been my help, and in the shadow of thy wings I sing for joy. My soul clings to thee; thy right hand upholds me. Ps. 63 vs. 1-8 "For God alone my soul waits in silence, from him comes my salvation. He only is my rock and salvation, my fortress, I shall not be greatly moved" Ps. 62 vs. 1 – 2

"Praise is due to thee, O God, in Zion; and to thee shall vows be performed, O thou who hearest prayer! To thee shall all flesh come on account of sins. When our transgressions prevail over us, thou dost forgive them. Blessed is he whom thou dost choose and bring near, to dwell in thy courts! We shall be satisfied with the goodness of thy house, thy holy temple! By dread deeds thou dost answer us with deliverance, O God of our salvation, who art the hope of all the ends of the earth, and of the farthest seas; who by thy strength hast established the mountains, being girded with might; who dost still the roaring of the seas, the roaring of the waves, the tumult of the peoples; so that those who dwell at earth's farthest bounds are afraid at thy signs; thou makest the outgoings of the morning and evening to shout for joy. Thou visitest the earth and waters it, thou greatly enrichest it; the river of God is full of water; thou providest their grain, for thou hast prepared it. Thou waterest its furrows abundantly, settling its ridges, softening it with showers, and blessing its growth. Thou crownest the year with thy bounty; the tracks of thy chariot drip with fatness. The pastures of the wilderness drip, the hills gird themselves with joy, the meadows clothe themselves with flocks, the valleys deck themselves with grain, they shout and sing together for joy." Ps. 65 vs. 1- 13

What a wonderful loving Father the Almighty God is. Do these beautiful lines of the above psalms not reveal to you God's tender loving fatherly kindness? Do not give Him lukewarm love, He hates it. He created you for love and desires to give you eternal life, a share in His Divine Life.

His precepts are easy if only you open your heart to Him and return love for love. Despite your sinfulness He is asking you to return to Him. Hearken to your heavenly Father's voice, cease from assisting your Father's enemy to hurt your Father who is suffering for your sake, delaying His coming as He desires to save as many souls as possible. He wants you to realize the need to detach yourself from Satan to have life eternal. He does not deserve your coldness, your nonchalant attitude, your disobedience and your ingratitude. Remember, He is suffering because He loves so much. He gave you all His love. It is true He owns Heaven, the world, yes, everything belongs to Him, but His Heart belongs to you. He was stripped of everything, He gave His last drop of Blood for you, why do you still hurt Him? Let His Priests and Bishops return to Him and serve him in humble obedience emulating our Lady for their reward is in Heaven and not in the transitory worldly pleasures and riches which lead to perdition. Certainly you are in the position to know better than your despiteful conduct. Shakespeare said "The eye sees not itself, but by reflection or by some other thing" why not advice one another on good conduct, how to combat the enemy who is at your heels. Certainly as shepherds of the flock of the Lord you must be capable to accept criticism in good faith as humble servants of the good Master who is Humility Himself. Failure to do this is nothing but pride. Think about it. The Lord is watching you in the eye. Today He is a Beggar, but tomorrow He will be the Judge when He comes in His glory. Make hay while the sun shines. If He came for you now are you ready to face Him?

CHAPTER XIV

INGRATITUDE

Is there any scientist, inventor, expeditioner or any one in his field of life who would remain unmoved if deprived of the rights of his discovery, invention or experimental results and allow someone else claim ownership of his achievement? Would he not rather make use of every legal resources at his disposal to shout to the top of the roof about his deprivation, proving his ownership, especially when this has to do with copy right and commercial benefits.

If we, being human, would not tolerate being deprived of our rights, what about God, the Lord of Heaven and Earth, whose Children we are, crying and reaching out for His children, pleading to possess what is rightfully His. He made you and me. We are His property and possession. Humanity did not evolve from anything. He is created by the Almighty God. Humanity is greatly favored to have stolen the Heart of God, as the nature of God is Love. Is it difficult to see the fatherly Love of the Almighty Father in His creation? Why is it difficult for atheists to acknowledge the existence of God, to open their heart to the God who created them and gave them His love? After all, the beauty of nature speaks about the Creator, sings to the glory of the one and only God, our Father in Heaven. It is impossible to be content with simply enjoying the creation without giving thought to the Creator. The creation did not create itself. There must be a Supreme Being, an Infinite Being responsible for the creation and this Infinite Supreme Being is the Almighty God, therefore, it is highly impossible not to believe in Him. The refusal to acknowledge His existence is blasphemy and inexcusable. God is a wonderful, awesome Father, the best Father. For love of you the Word became Flesh for you to reach Him, paid for your sins to give you eternal life. The whole creation portrays His Beauty, His love, for only a most loving Father can create such a beautiful world for His Children with such variety of nutrition for their nourishment. He stands at the door of your heart and knocks, waiting patiently to be let in for Him to help you realize He loves you. Do not keep Him waiting, act while the sun shines!

How astonishingly true, those who have tasted the Goodness of our Lord, those who know Him and serve Him, who are expected to live exemplary life are those who hurt Him the most. They are Judases of today, betraying their Master with a kiss. Such are the clergy and Bishops, who are obsessed with the accumulation of worldly riches contrary to the Will of their Divine Master who, during His earthly life, had no earthly possession, even the sepulcher, His burial place, did not belong to Him. He lived poor and died poor to enter into His Glory. The followers of Jesus Christ, the Divine Master, have no earthly possession. Jesus made it clear His Kingdom is not of this world. He is the King of Love, King of Glory, King of Heaven therefore, His followers, though they be in the world yet they are not of the world. With this on mind their reward is in Heaven, the Kingdom of their Master, their eternal Home. These Judases stain the image of true friends of Jesus, the image of those who are faithful to their vocation. If one says yes to his call one should remain faithful to it. Unfaithfulness is ingratitude to the Grace bestowed on one. Jesus has accomplished his redemptive mission therefore, He does not need another Judas to pave way to it. However, the Judases of today betray Jesus to their own disadvantage as they hinder themselves from the entrance into the Kingdom which the Father lovingly wants to give them. Nevertheless, it would be wise to return with genuine repentance to the Most Merciful Savior. The Sacrament of Reconciliation is at your disposal however, He did not institute it for one to become a swine of iniquity. It is a Sacrament of His love to go and sin no more. Jesus did not fall down intentionally while carrying the cross. It would be a grievous mistake to deceive oneself as God cannot be deceived. The Sacrament of Reconciliation is Holy and must be treated as such. Your Divine Master is calling you to return before it is too late for a wise decision. Satan, the arch enemy, is bent on the ruin of souls, therefore, return to your Master when you still have the possibility. Judas had ample opportunities to refrain from the betrayal of his Master and Friend, but he would not, due to greed, until it was too late for sane decision, though he repented, but having exposed himself to Satan pride became his inevitable option resulting in suicide.

Being aware the media is one of the instruments of Satan against the Church, the people of God should equip themselves with the amour of God and prove themselves capable to the task of disappointing the enemy by not supplying the media what they are eagerly expecting, the slightest misconduct, to tarnish the image of the Church which is the Body of Christ. They would exaggerate what they get to cause much ado about nothing and make a mountain out of an Ant hill. For this reason great caution is expected of the Bishops and clergy as they are open letters and spiritual guide of the Faithful. It is very disappointing, the misconduct of the Bishop of Limburg in Germany who betrayed His Divine Master because of worldly possession. In his insatiable desire to acquire for himself the luxury of living in a palace, in this transitory world, although His Divine Master, during His earthly life, never had one, forgot the effect it would have on the Flock entrusted into his care.

His disgusting misconduct coupled with that of some of his counterparts led to a large number of Catholics deviating from their Faith. Nonetheless, any Catholic who deviates due to the misconduct of a Priest or Bishop is not worthy of God's love. One is not a Catholic because of the clergy or the Bishop but because of Jesus the God-Man Who shed His Most Precious Blood for love of us to found His Church, the One, Holy, Catholic and Apostolic Church. One is a Catholic Christian because one loves God and believes in Jesus Christ. The One, Holy, Catholic and Apostolic Church, the Body of Jesus, the new Israel, a Family, is Holy, even though Her members are sinners, She saves. Jesus is aware of the sinful nature of the members of His Mystical Body. The Church is alive, Her Soul is the Holy Spirit. It is not worth it, to lose Heaven because of the misconduct of a Priest or Bishop. It is wise to remain in the Church, for the love of Jesus, trusting in Him who is Faithful and Trustworthy. Nevertheless, the Bishop of Limburg should have known better than the pipe he played as the pomp and riches of this world has no relationship with a servant of God. He should have counted his teeth with his tongue. Does the luxury of this world worth the loss of Heaven? Is it wise to betray your Master with a thing of transient? You fed and nourished the media with their favorite dish at the expense of your Divine Master who is in agony. Offences must come but woe to Him through whom offenses come. May humanity have pity on He Who came to give us life not death. Love your God!

Another thing to be called to mind by all the Faithful is the value of family. The One Holy, Catholic and Apostolic Church is a Family, Mother, Bride and Body of Jesus Christ. The Church for whose sake He shed His most Precious Blood to found is a Family. She is an Organism, She is alive and She has feelings. Due to its authenticity it does not matter how often this fact is emphasized hence the Church as Mother and Body of the Divine feeds the soul with Divine nourishment which She alone possesses in the Sacrament of the Eucharist, the source and summit of the Catholic Faith, whereby the soul receives Jesus Christ Himself, Body, Blood, Soul and Divinity, and is consequently gradually transformed into Jesus Christ to share His Divine Life with Him, for Him and in Him eternally in eternity. This Church which Jesus founded also provides true and complete doctrine for all Christians. The destiny of a large number of souls after this mortal body is at stake, Satan is struggling hard to mislead them for perdition, therefore be vigilant. The Catholic Church, the Body of Jesus Christ, is the Vine, and all the Christians are the branches. Anyone who leaves the Church, for reasons best known to him, cuts himself automatically off from the Vine and risks the chance of making Heaven, unless it is not as a result of his own fault or he dies as a martyr. But would you want to take such a gamble for your salvation? Jesus strictly instructed and prayed that "they may be one" meaning members of His mystical Body should, under no circumstance, separate. He came to find and save what was lost. Everyone is a sinner not a judge. Jesus alone is the Judge. The Divine Master wishes both the righteous and the sinner to remain together until the time of harvest when the Angels will collect the wheats and burn the weeds.

As the Church of God is a Family every member is expected to treat Her as such bearing on mind She is the Body of Jesus Christ. There is no need pointing accusing finger at the Church to which you belong, but rather pray for Her well-being, for the well-being of your Family who is Jesus Christ. What happens in the Family remains within the Family. It does not matter how ugly that may seem, Jesus sees it all. He is aware of it all. Should you find whatever offends you unbearable consult Jesus in prayer, make use of the Sacrament of reconciliation you will definitely find consolation. He surely will grant you the Grace to bear it for love of Him, after all He is the ultimate Goal and justice is His. Taking the weakness of the Clergy and Bishops to the media, either for material compensation or to draw attention to your person, does not portray you better than those you intend to expose. In so doing you are exposing Jesus Who sacrificed Himself on the cross for your salvation merely because you would not carry your cross and follow Him. Is there anything one cannot bear for the love of such a wonderful God? Before running to the media one should have had a thorough examination of conscience in order to verify if ones Christianity depends on the conduct of the ministers of the Church or on ones love for the God who loves him infinitely, shed His Most Precious Blood for his salvation and wants to see him in Heaven for eternal life with Him. If you were a faithful Catholic and knew your Faith, then you must have realized that exposing the Family is exposing yourself, therefore, this would have made you disappoint the enemy, inform Jesus in prayer and allow Him take care of the situation.

Do you not have faith in God? Don't you have a personal relationship with Jesus? Don't you realize He lives in you? Don't you realize you can talk with Him every time? Is He not there for you in the Tabernacle? Don't you receive Him worthily in the Eucharist? Why not make use of the Confessional? Don't you realize you can inform the Pope if you lost faith in your Priest and in your Bishop? Have pity on your God, be patient with Him and love Him.

Consequent to the incident of the Bishop of Limburg, concerning the exorbitant price for his luxurious palace, some Catholics informed the media their intention to desert the Church, talking to the instrument of the enemy against their Lord and Savior Jesus Christ Who is the Church. The Church is His Body. One would have expected to hear their resolution to be more deeply devoted to Jesus and His Church. This way they would have proved themselves true Catholics, consequently put the enemy to shame. Jesus would have been pleased. They would have gained for themselves some special Grace rather than cause Him and our Lady so much tears. It is not God's Will that anyone should perish. Jesus desires everyone to be saved, but He cannot seize our freewill. He sheds Holy tears for so many souls who would perish. It is not enough to be Catholic without practicing your Faith. Jesus expects you to be Catholic very well acquainted with your Catholic Faith. Please do remember, the Bishops and the Priests are there to administer the Sacraments and to feed the Faithful with the word of God. Everyone must give an account of his life to God. Gods infinite love for each one of us does not depend on the merit of anyone, therefore, why must your love for Him depend on some minister's conduct? Love bears all things. If Jesus is loved genuinely for Who He is, there is nothing whatsoever that can make that love falter. A genuine love for God makes you overlook all odds, observe His precepts and carry your cross patiently. Is there any cross you may carry greater than the One He carried for love of you? Why not bear this little for Him? Should all the Clergy betray Him you would pity Him, remain in His Church, always aware He gave His life for Her because He loves Her infinitely. For this reason you will defend Her even if it caused you your life. God is Love, Jesus is Love, therefore be love. You are created for Love and for love. Love is the answer. Ask Him for the Grace to be patient, He will grant it you. But bear on mind, we cannot change God, rather we should become docile for Him to transform us for Himself.

A sinner is, as is well known, someone who takes delight in committing sin. Whoever says he is a servant of Jesus Christ must avoid sin, otherwise, he has no share in Him. Jesus hates sin. In His own words "He who commits sin is of the devil; for the devil has sinned from the beginning" 1st Jn 3 vs 8. Therefore, it is most absurd for anyone who calls himself a minister of God to support sin. One God, One Church, one Baptism. A branch which has been cut down from a tree does not belong to the tree any more. Therefore, the protestant churches who cut themselves from the Vine, from His Holy Church, do not belong to the vine any longer. This is not passing judgement but rather a reminder of the truth of God. "I am the Vine and you are the branches" Jesus said "I do not pray for these only, but also for those who will believe in me through their word, that they may all be one; even as thou, Father, art in me, and I in thee, that they also may be in us, so that the world may believe that thou hast sent me." Jn 17 vs 20 – 21. To be one is to remain together as one Body, one Church, one Baptism, subject to Peter, the Pope, the Vicar of Jesus Christ on Earth. Jesus did not pray for churches or divisions in His Church rather for unity. There is only one true God, a Trinitarian God, so the Church with so many members should be One just as the Holy Trinity is One God. "If you love me keep my commandment" breaking away from the Vine does not portray obedience to the Beloved Savior.

How can ecumenism work when those who separated themselves are not making enough effort to this effect. They do not only ordain women pastors but also bishops. As though that is not enough they support and encourage sin. Why willfully trade on dangerous ground? "But I warn you whom to fear; fear him who, after he has killed, has power to cast into hell; yes I tell you, fear him" A clear warning from Jesus to those who indulge in sin, to those who encourage sin and put a deaf ear to His appeal for holiness. A warning to those who engage in promiscuous sexual life, those who do not observe His commandments and do not abide in His love. Those who have drowned themselves in mortal sin. Do they not realize to condone same sex marriage and homosexuality is an affront, a slap on the Face of Jesus, crucifying Him all over again, this time extremely more cruel than the executioners who were ignorant of His Divinity. This is ingratitude in its extremity from those who said they know Him. For an evangelical pastor, Nikolaus Schneider, the chairman of their synod, to proudly announce to the media his disgusting act of granting homosexual couple church wedding, which is against the Christian norms, is very unwise an absurd.

It is sacrilegious! Which Jesus is he serving anyway? What is the meaning of church wedding? Does he expect Jesus to bless such a wedding? Does he not realize such an act is an insolence to the Almighty God! How could he dare go against God's Law? Does common sense alone not tell him and his fellow clergy they are not in tune with God's law and as such could not possibly be delivering sound doctrine to the children of God. The God of Creation, who holds Heaven and Earth in His hands, Alfa and Omega, Author and Giver of Life, King of Glory, gave commandments governing the inhabitants of the earth He created. Surely, He expects His commandments to be honored and not for man to make an alternative against His Holy Will. One cannot serve God and mammon. To condone sin, the very reason for which the Son of God shed His Most Precious Blood, and at the same time grant this sin the blessing of the church, is indeed disgusting. Does he not know homosexuality and the like are sins from hell? If they were true disciples of Jesus, His true ministers, definitely they would have known the pain they cause Him. Not only did they tear His Body apart, with their segregation, they now support His enemy, Satan, openly. The point is, ..."by their fruits ye shall know them", to be a church minister is for them a professional attraction and social status than carrying out the Holy Will of the Almighty God. Unfortunately, one cannot help but sympathize with their members who are scape goats of the folly of their ministers. But on the other hand, humanity is favored with intellect, to detect good from evil, therefore one must be aware that "When a blind man leads the blind both will fall into the pit" The one and only true Church of God, the One, Holy, Catholic and Apostolic Church founded by Jesus on Peter would never encourage same-sex relationships nor grant it a Church wedding because the Holy Spirit is the Soul of the Church. One should never forget one would someday confront God face to face.

However, that notwithstanding, we have a most wonderful and most merciful God. Despite our sinfulness He loves us infinitely and waits patiently for our return. It is entirely our own choice to accept or reject the God of Love who would stop at nothing for our happiness. The day is still young, but the night is fast approaching, to accept His Divine Mercy or face His judgement. Our good Lord would prefer to show Mercy and not judgement because we are His beloved children. He is God, He cannot be less than He is. He cannot change His nature. We have to allow Him mold us to suit Him so as to enable us share His Divine Life with Him. He is a God of Love, Mercy and Justice. Have pity on your God who created you, loves you as His children with a motherly love. Turn from your wicked ways, repent and embrace the Father's love and have life.

CHAPTER XV

THE BEAUTY OF MOTHERHOOD

God in His infinite Wisdom and Goodness created woman from the rib of man as he was asleep. Woman thus became the beauty of man, his companion. Their union meant to express the beauty of God's Love whose innermost being is Love. However, this design of God was not allowed to blossom, as it was sabotaged by Satan who deceived the woman Eve, consequently leading to the fall of man. Little did Adam realize his love for Eve would have been beautifully enriched had he loved God, his Creator more than he did Eve. He would not have failed woefully. It was originally Gods intention for Adam to love his wife, Eve, as he loved himself to portray Gods nature, Love, but it was not for him to make the grievous mistake of giving his heart more to Eve than to God, an unthoughtful error that led to his ultimate loss of his relationship with God. His disloyalty to God robed him the paradise he would still have retained, while loving his Eve, had he acted otherwise. The triangular relationship between man, woman and God failed because God was given second place, thereby paving way for the penetration of an outside stimuli, Satan, which ultimately lead to the fall of man to the disappointment of God.

However, God had other plans, a new Adam and a new Eve who would love Him above everything and assist Him to realize His Vision with humanity on whom He lost His Heart, on whom He intends to lavish His love. A new Adam and a new Eve who would be faithful and trustworthy, whose love for Him transcends death. A perfect Eve, the model of womanhood, who would trust in His love for her, a love which transcends the sacrifice of her only son "I am the handmaid of the Lord, be it done unto me according to thy word" whose "heart would be pierced with a sword" yet her faith, love and trust in God remains unshakable. Adam and Eve, who, united in love, yet each loving God the Father above the other. For the purpose of the new Adam the Word took Flesh in the new Eve who believed that what was said to her by Angel Gabriel would be fulfilled. Mary, the humble hand maid of God, who by her "Yes" to God portrays the beauty of motherhood, paving way for the new Adam. Her perfection in her role as the Mother of the only begotten Son of God, Her humble trust in God's love, even if she did not understand, is the beauty of motherhood. The Almighty God has special love for a woman whom he formed after His nature, for as Father, He has a motherly love for humanity. Every woman has a special role, a unique role as mother to play either in a family as a mother or in a consecrated life as a bride of Christ. The beauty of motherhood can only be realized if based on Mary as the Model, then will there be fulfillment. A woman is the mother of the nation. Every woman is a mother and should be respected. To respect a woman is to respect God in awe of Who He is in His Creation.

Each time I behold a mother with her child my heart soars high with joy as I remember the Incarnation of the Holy Child Jesus. Such moments enable me visualize the blessed Virgin Mary holding her Divine child Jesus in her arms. This great mystery of the Incarnation, the Word made Flesh in the blessed Virgin's womb, the Ark of God, is a tremendous conveyance of Gods attachment to humanity. The God of Creation became vulnerable, touchable, reachable, nourished with a mother's milk, learnt to sit, stand, walk and dwelt among His creatures as one of them. What a marvelous miraculous act of Grace on humanity, for the Holy Trinity, God of Creation to take Flesh in the second person of the Holy Trinity, in the womb of the blessed Virgin Mary to make atonement for sin, reconcile with humanity and restore to humanity the glory that was hers from the foundation of the world. This beautiful, sweet Incarnation of God in Jesus Christ deserves, unceasingly, all praise and all thanksgiving from every human soul in gratitude for the abundant life granted to man through the ultimate sacrifice of the Innocent Lamb of God for the redemption of man from original sin, inherited from the first parents Adam and Eve. After all, the least humanity can do for this priceless gesture of the Divine is to have a grateful heart, to be in constant expression of gratitude to the God of Love for His infinite Mercy, for His most Merciful Love.

Motherhood in itself is beautiful, more so as it reflects the beauty of the Incarnation of the Son of God. If only mothers would realize the gift of motherhood, which possesses a flair of Divinity, as it portrays the nature of Gods fatherly loving relationship to man, then, every mother would value being a mother with all intention for perfection, focusing on Mary as her role Model. Every woman is a mother, every mother is Mary and mother of Jesus Christ in her own child, therefore, a model to society, whereby she models her life in the fashion of Mary the blessed Virgin, being to her own child what Mary was to Jesus, educating her child in the precepts of God in loving obedience, embracing her motherhood as her vocation in humble trust to the Holy Will of God in the sacrifice of self. Gods special love for woman, designed for her in her motherhood, is an ornament of adornment bestowed on humanity, perfectly demonstrated in His masterpiece creation of the Blessed Virgin Mary whose "Yes", in that very instant, made the Word take Flesh in her womb, consequently making the invincible God, though still invincible, visible in Jesus Christ. This beautiful Incarnation of the Son of God was made possible for the salvation of humanity through motherhood which can only realize its full beauty if modelled on the Blessed Virgin Mary who, Herself, is motherhood in perfection. It is only in so doing will there be a fulfilment in motherhood, the mirror of Gods loving nature for humanity. Bearing on mind, a mother's love derives its beauty from the Divine, there is the need for every mother to be in constant awareness of this beautiful Divine attribute she possesses, so as to raise up children in the footsteps of Jesus Christ for a healthy society pleasing to God. A woman, therefore is the darling of the Father, created for His Glory in a special way. To be aware of this reality is a beauty therapy, for every woman, as it enhances the beauty of her soul which reflects in the glow of her face. This ultimately cancels the need for beauty creams and cosmetic surgery, as she surrenders her will to God, to Jesus Christ, for perfect peace and tranquility.

Unfortunately this beautiful reality has been overshadowed by the urge in most women, to rub shoulders with the masculine world, whereby the essence of motherhood is undermined with the pursuit of professional status, in their quest for financial independence from men, placing themselves in defiance to the natural set-up of Providence for raising up children morally stable for a healthy society. It is not a surprise however, the dilemma of the world today in her inability to control the rampant crimes which are dished to her by the moral decay of her children. When mothers are no more what they should be, selfishly dumping their children in boarding schools and nursery schools in pursuit of their career, nothing better should be expected.

Furthermore, the indifference, the contempt of God to whom humanity owes her existence has become a parasite that tends to drain the world of all that is good for a healthy society. This unpleasant situation, nevertheless could be overcome if humanity turned to her Creator who is God, who alone has the cure for the problems facing the world today. God, our Creator, in His infinite Goodness, yearns for each individual to accept His Divine Mercy and come back to Him like the prodigal son in order to find peace. God is God, the one and only God Who holds the world in His Hands, Who has the solution to every problem the world faces, beckons everyone into His loving fatherly Arms to find rest, for the healing of the world. What a loving Father of humanity God is! A friend and lover of man. The enemy of the world is Satan, he blinds the world, he is the cause of all the problems of the world, an impostor, a liar, deceitful, a camouflage, making man point accusing fingers at God Who is infinite Goodness, for the errors and hardships in the world for which he alone is responsible.

How shocking and terrifying it would be, at death, to discover, on the long run, the result of the grievous error of giving a deaf ear to the voice of God, when one is confronted with the reality of hell, the eternal home of Satan and unrepentant sinners. Then it would be too late to put back the clock. It is very unwise to trade your eternal happiness, in the Fathers Kingdom, for perdition. Why would you want to hurt such a loving Father as God, the One and only God Who created you with love in his own image, in a unique way, endowed you with talents, provided you with a beautiful world in which to exist to know Him, serve Him and finally come back to Him to share in His divine life in Heaven. A God of love, who chose to call you His child and not His slave. Why would you want to hurt such a loving Father. Why should He be allowed to have sorrow, to be in constant agony? Why would you cause your Father, the Almighty God to shed tears? Parents know the pain they have when they lose their child, who do not belong to them rather entrusted to them by God, although some may not know this, to help them learn about Him and to love Him. Children belong to God, so does everyone. Nevertheless, although parents grieve at the loss of their children, who do not actually belong to them, yet men fail to realize God feels pain for every unrepentant sinner who sends himself to hell for then he is dead. God, his real parent who would have loved to pamper him eternally in Eternity, weeps at his loss. God weeps over such sinners.

It is indeed sad to realize most women, who should be humble mothers, like Mary, being to their husbands what Mary was to St. Joseph, her husband, encouraging them to sane reasoning in keeping the Holy Will of God, are those, in their arrogance, make a show of equality with men. In their pursuit of women liberation and social status, a display in the political arena, they take the lead in breaking Gods law. Their conscience sold, they support abortion, same sex marriage, euthanasia, test-tube babies, encouraging cloning and the like. Don't these women realize it is their place to voice out the evils encouraged by the men? Why would they support the evil practices of things which humiliate women, things against natural law that offend God? No one has a right to decide on who should live and who should not, except God the Author and Giver of life, the Eternal Father, Creator of all that is. If women realized their dignity as women, according to the design of Providence, they would have been instruments of peace in their respective homes, winning their husbands over to keep their focus on God and observe His precepts for a better world. The practice of euthanasia on adults is alarming, an offence to God. That notwithstanding the governments of this world are beginning to extend that to innocent children. These children, in their ailments, are children of God, they are loved by God, yet despite their ailment God did not permit any one to kill them. It should be understood, God loves every individual uniquely and has a purpose for every one sick or whole therefore, it is a mortal sin to put an end to life despite ailments. How would you know about the souls of those innocent babies? Do you know their relationship with God? Besides, whatever God allows is for a purpose. God's Holy Will is love and Mercy itself. God alone has an answer to everything, why not ask Him Who is more than willing to guide and direct you. Everyone has to carry his cross and follow Jesus Christ. To eliminate the cross for the incapability to bear it is not the answer. There is strength in the cross of Jesus Christ of Nazareth, keep focus on it.

He Who offered Himself in sacrifice for the redemption of humanity has answers to every problem. Look to Him Who opened the gate of Heaven for all to go in and have Eternal life. One should refrain from wrong doing, accept Divine life, in Jesus Christ the Beloved Redeemer.

CHAPTER XVI

INTERFERENCE

Disobedience, what a word! a most distasteful word to every level headed parent whose sole objective is to raise up healthy and morally stable children. Parents, of course would want to do this in accordance to their respective precepts. These parents desire to raise up subordinate children who would grow up to their expectation, consequently, be the joy of their heart, the pride of their parenthood. However, should these children be less than their expectation, what if they misconstrued their good intentions to see them grow up into well behaved children for a healthy society, turned disobedient, no longer sane, instigated by selfishness, the product of misconception, inconsideration, consequently yielded to disillusion, accusation of parents wanting in parental love, which eventually results to the children being indifferent to the feelings of their parents, would that not break their parents heart?. Definitely, these parents would not help but shed secret tears, wondering at their children's blindness to the deep love they have for them, their concern for their future happiness in adulthood.

Would it not be quite natural for these unfortunate parents to expect sympathy from any outsider who happens to be informed about their dilemma. If human parents would feel this way over children who actually do not belong to them, but entrusted to their care by the Almighty Father who is the Creator and Father of humanity, how much more would He feel over the disobedience and blindness of the children He created in His own image with love and for love. How would He feel to their estrangement? What other way should this God prove His love for mankind, having offered His only begotten Son in sacrifice for the love of man. Do not forget the God-Head suffered for humanity. While the Son went through His bitter passion, the torture in the Flesh, the Father and the Holy Spirit who live in the Son suffered with Him. God has been suffering because He loves humanity, otherwise He is self-content and wouldn't have had any course to suffer. He does not desire any single human soul to perish. He is in agony for the stubbornness and blindness of humanity. This God Who left His heavenly abode where Cherubim and Seraphim prostrate without ceasing before Him, the God of Creation, the Supreme Being, Author and Giver of life, God of Glory, to become man, stripping Himself of every luxury, taking upon Himself the wages of sin, He who had no sin, to be tortured in a most cruel manner never before heard of nor would ever be heard of. Even the worst criminal was never tortured as He was, imprisoned, chained, scourged, mocked, crowned with thorns, unjustly tried, condemned and finally crucified like a criminal, would you not have pity on Him? All these He bore in silence for His infinite love for humanity. How is He expected to feel when man turns round to say he is not loved by God? How else should our good Lord Jesus Christ make us realize His Most Sacred Heart is a burning Furnace of Love and He is being consumed for His Love for humanity? The God of Love is in agony, in great agony, weeping for the unrequited love of His estranged children who are heading for perdition on their own free will.

That notwithstanding, politicians have taken it into their hands to tumble God's plan for the existence of humanity on this planet earth. They tend to forget the Almighty God put them in that office for the maintenance of law and order and to see to the proper sharing of worldly goods, bearing on mind the needs of the poor. The Almighty God, Lord of Heaven and Earth has interest in what goes on in the world He created. One should therefore, not assume otherwise and misinterpret His silence for weakness. On the contrary, it is love, yes indeed love, the God of love in His infinite Mercy opened up the ocean of His Divine Mercy to mankind, an effort to save as many souls as possible from perdition before His second coming as a Judge. Therefore, anyone who values his life should wake up and be wise and accept the Lord's Divine Mercy, turn a new leaf, sincerely repenting for offending the Almighty Father, in order to spend Eternity in Heaven eternally in Jesus, with Jesus and for Jesus.

However, it must be called to mind that the government of this world and the Church of God have nothing in common. They are two autonomous bodies therefore, the politicians cannot dictate to the Church. The Church is the Body of Christ and as such not of this world but Heavenly. The One, Holy, Catholic and Apostolic Church whose head is Jesus Christ led by His Vicar the Pope is not a worldly institution. She is organic, a Person, Jesus Christ. The Church is the Bride of Christ, a Mother and the Holy Spirit is Her Soul. The Church is Holy. The fact that Her members are sinners does not make Her less Holy. Her Founder is Holy, the second Person of the Holy Trinity, Jesus Christ the Son of the Eternal Father. The only authority to admonish the ministers of the Church is Jesus Christ Himself not the politicians. It is wisdom to obey God rather than man. According to Jesus the tares and the wheat should be allowed to grow together so as not to uproot the wheat while uprooting the tares. This task is for the Angels, the tares have been planted by the enemy. Therefore, the united nations have no right whatsoever to dictate to the Vatican what is right and what is not. The Vatican has the truth of God and must listen to the Holy Spirit who rules and governs the Church. The Church is not of the world, although in the world yet, she has the commandments of God, the Sacraments instituted by Jesus Christ Himself, for the sanctification of her members. One would expect the united nations to focus their attention in solving the problems in the world which are becoming a threat to the peace of the world and cease to interfere in the affairs of the Church being mindful of offending God.

Nevertheless, it should not be mistaken, unless the world leaders recognize the Supremacy of God, turn to the Most Sacred Heart of Jesus for refuge, appreciate His Divine Mercy, the world peace would remain an illusion. In these times, the order of the day seems to be greed by selfish leaders who are drunk with power, living as though the world belongs to them, indifferent to the feelings of their subjects who elected them on the strength of the promises they made to them during their campaign. As soon as these leaders achieve their political aspirations they begin to act as though they are immortal, accumulating for themselves worldly goods, blinded by greed and self-esteem to the disadvantage of their subjects who elected them in the hope for a better tomorrow. These greedy leaders who deprive the poor adequate share of the natural resources provided for all by the Good God to Whom everything and everyone belong, fail to realize they would someday leave their mortal bodies to face the Almighty God whose Law they so defy, without conscience. Why should they be deaf to the cry of their subjects who express their disappointments, who use the only possible means at their disposal, demonstration, to be heard and cared for. A leader is a father to his subjects not a tyrant, not a dictator.

It is most unfortunate that peaceful demonstrations are made to escalate, causing loss of lives and in some cases result to civil war, merely because power-stricken leaders would not step down for new elections. They would rather take to forceful means to disperse peaceful demonstrations. The fact God created man in His own image is a guarantee every individual is in possession of a soul, conscience and intellect therefore, capable of differentiating evil from good. God, the infinite Goodness and Love, Merciful and Just, expects to see Himself in mankind who are His children. Taking to forceful means in order to retain power is an evidence of rejecting the Good and choosing the bad. There are two forces present in the world, Good and evil, the later of course relating to Satan the source of wickedness, the enemy of God and mankind. These leaders, void in love, should be pitied as power drunkenness portrays the depth of a sick soul on the verge of perdition who can only obtain cure if they turned to the physician of the soul Who is no one else but the God of Love, Jesus Christ, Who in His infinite Mercy would be glad to welcome them and grant them the peace they lack if they showed genuine repentance.

However, it never rains but it purrs. It is indeed sad to see how man continues to deviate, with all consciousness, from the precepts of God, provoking the God of Love, the long suffering, patient God waiting for the world to recognize His love and have pity on a Father shedding tears of sorrow, a Father in agony, yearning for the love of His estranged children. What has the Almighty Father not done for mankind to prove His love for them. The one thing God hates is sin and yet, He humbled Himself, became sin for our transgression, paid the price of sin in His only begotten Son, Jesus Christ, on the cross of cavalry, for love of humanity. Jesus died on the cross after having been extremely tortured by mankind, blinded as they were, incapable of realizing it was their Creator, their God, they were so brutally torturing, yet Jesus bore it all in silence to please His Father and to give life to humanity. This most Beloved Jesus, Lover of mankind, is not allowed by mankind, for whose love He gave up His life, in the most bitter manner, under such extreme pain, such cruel torture on the cross, to stop weeping. Yes, Jesus weeps over the loss of so many souls who would end up in perdition because they are His children. It is sad to see the nations of this world indulging in the very sins for which He gave His life for the salvation of mankind. Nations after nations legalizing abominations in the name of modernization, thereby permitting the promiscuousness of sin and hurting God. When the ruling class are deficient in sound reasoning one is left to ponder at the capability of such rulers to maintain a healthy and decent society. One has not yet recuperated from the shock of supporting and legalizing abortion they dropped another bomb, the legalization of murder in the name of euthanasia, leaving one to wonder what the world is turning into.

Today being gay has become fashionable. That a man or woman would publicly disclose, proudly, he is gay or she is lesbian, without conscience, without the fear of God, unaware of the reality of being a living corpse is indeed most pitiable. Those who indulge in such sinful life-style should be aware, unless there is genuine repentance, the divine Mercy of God embraced, their souls would not escape perdition. Have the politicians lost their direction by making themselves the instruments of Satan and dare to be defiance to the ordinances of God. Woe to you politicians who have become the Pharisees of modern times who would not enter through the door and yet prevent others from entering through it, acting contrary to your call, assuming to know better than the God who put you in that position for His purpose, to whom you must surely give an account of how you managed what was entrusted to you. One thing so loving about our God is His Goodness, His Divine Mercy and His patience, always ready to receive every repentant sinner. The door of His Divine Mercy is wide open for sinners, the greater the sins the more right to His Mercy therefore, make hay while the sun shines, turn new leaves, make haste to open the door of your heart to Jesus Who is tenderly knocking, begging for you to return to Him, while He yet delays His coming as a righteous Judge.

Perhaps, one can call Africa to mind, her days when nothing was known about her. When she was known as the dark continent, which consequently made her an attraction for Europe, arousing in Europeans the spirit of adventure into the unknown, to discover, and Christianize the inhabitants of the dark continent, having been themselves favored by the Almighty God to embrace Christianity first. But today one cannot help but purse to wonder at what has become of Europe with her Christian ethics. Has time turned the pupils into teachers and teachers into pupils? Those who were said to be uncultivated, uncivilized, lacking in the knowledge of God and of His Christ, evangelized by the sons of Europe, how is it they are the ones now teaching Europeans the bearing in relation to nature, to what is sound, as would be pleasing to Almighty God who made Europe what she is today? Has technology resulted to Europe's blindness, deafness, lack of conscience to the precepts of God, the Creator of this beautiful world with all her resources for the comfort of humanity in whom He instilled natural laws for existence. Has science, granted by Providence, an irrefutable source of proof of the existence of God, which portrays the awesomeness of His Beauty and Wisdom, made Europe blind, arrogant, resulting to degeneration, turning her great knowledge to illiteracy. It is definitely absurd for Europe and America to make much ado about nothing over the fact African countries strongly oppose same-sex relationships. How could one expect matrimony, a holy sacrament, instituted by Jesus Christ Himself between male and female to be conferred to man and man and otherwise. What an abomination!

As though that was not enough Belgium passed a law legalizing murder on innocent children in the pretext of relieving them from severe suffering. What right have politicians, who pass such laws, to the life of human beings whose number of hair they cannot count. They should not forget these innocent children belong to God Who created them and sent them into this world for a purpose. God did not ask for their help. Euthanasia has now become the order of the day. Since 2000 this evil is being practiced on adults in the Netherland and in some other parts of Europe. Such sins, same sex relationships, abortion, transvestites and so on, are indirectly being imposed on Africa by Europe. They thus create the impression they want Africa to bear the consequence of defying God's natural Law for humanity with them. How wrong they are! Africa is in her underdevelopment wiser than presumed. When it comes to moral issues their conscience is intact. For the African is such sinful practices of Europe abomination. However, one may dare ask, is such moral decay Europe's way of showing gratitude to the Almighty Father for all her benefits? Why send souls, who would perhaps have been saved if they endured their purging and bear their cross with faith and trust in the Lord Jesus Christ, to perdition, by encouraging them commit suicide which is mortal sin. Perhaps, they would have had the chance of conversion or they would have been a means of the conversion of family members or someone else. The Almighty Father is Lord of Creation, a loving Father He is aware of all the human sufferings. All there is to it is simply to trust in Him then one would gradually begin to understand the meaning of suffering and love. There must be suffering otherwise the Lord Jesus would not have exposed Himself to such extreme suffering beyond comparison. A father who chastises his child loves his child as he would want his child to possess good virtues. The Holy Bible emphasizes the need to chastise the child "Spare the rod and spoil the child." The Almighty Father, the Supreme Authority, Who is Love, created humanity with love and for love, as a loving Father struggling to save His children from perdition, does chastise to call mankind to reason and draw their attention to Himself, therefore He allows suffering, but He does not cause suffering.

The touch of tsunamis, storm, tornados, or lightning, which are meant to instigate humanity give a thought to eternal life, seek his God and return to Him who is the Author and Giver of life, unfortunately produce, in most cases, the opposite effect portraying the depth, the enemy, Satan, has injected his venom in mankind, creating wrong impression of the Beloved heavenly Father so that the Eternal Father, Who is Love, is accused of lack of love as a result of many lives lost in such incidents including innocent children. But one tends to forget the Almighty Father's desire to have all His children with Him in Heaven, so He must have made provision for every single soul affected. This world expires, it is but wise to make provision for a lasting abode eternally with the Eternal Father in Heaven. Hear His voice, turn new leaves, keep God's precepts when His arms are wide open for embrace in His Divine Mercy. Better be wise, do not trade where Angels fear to trade, while the sun shines.

> Awake O Soul, consider your wretchedness
> Seek Him who covers your wretchedness
> With such tremendous infinite love, therefore,
> Refrain from your waywardness, Accept Him
> Who is your peace, the long sought peace.

Do not say I know Him, His benefits I have enjoyed. Fall not back into ways left behind. Be steadfast in His precepts. Trust in Him Who is able to sustain you. For Him is now, not then, the ultimate state for the promised Land, the Eternal Home of the Beloved.

CHAPTER XVII

CONCLUSION

Considering the turmoil in the world today, the power drunkenness of world leaders who misuse their office, acting as though they own the world, immune to the feelings of their subjects, who want to lord it over their subjects for life, one begins to wonder at their capability for true human feelings. They would not hesitate to demonstrate power over their unfortunate subjects with their military arsenal oblivious of the fact they are created beings clothed with mortality. Why make war, causing the death of another, because you want to rule over him against his will. Do you not realize everyone in this world are brothers and sisters, children of the Almighty God? Despite the different nationalities, races and belief the inhabitants of this world are one Folk. Do you not realize that as children of God, wherever we find ourselves is our home and country because the world belongs to God Who is our Father. We must love and respect one another regardless of social status. Jesus taught us this. His Incarnation, life and resurrection has united all peoples together, as one, in Him. Thus He revealed our identity, children of God Who are Love. Love should reign in every heart. There is no need creating demarcations trying to know where someone you meet comes from, it leads to racial discrimination, rather simply treat him as a brother, for he is a child of God just like you. He is a human being like you, that is all there is to it, having the same identity as you, God's child. The world belongs to the universal Father, the Almighty God. In Heaven, there is only one Folk, one Family, a colorful wonderful Family of God. Demarcation does not exist, Love reigns. So, Love must also reign on earth. God wills it.

How could anyone dare violate the commandment of God to "love your neighbor as yourself" How could Putin dare violate international convention to seize Crimea for amalgamation to Russia, undermining the opinion of Ukraine to which she belongs. Does it not occur to him he might be provoking the wrath of God on himself? Does he think his very life belongs to him? What would he do if his life is demanded of him by God to whom his life belongs? This goes to all the world leaders in the same category and everyone who puts his trust in his worldly possessions as an instrument to trample on the less favored. Consider once more this parable of our good Lord to whom this world belongs "The land of a rich man brought forth plentifully; and he thought to himself, 'what shall I do, for I have nowhere to store my crops?' And he said, 'I will do this: I will pull down my barns, and build larger ones; and there I will store all my grain and my goods. And I will say to my Soul, you have ample goods laid up for many years; take your ease, eat, drink, be merry.' But God said to him, 'Fool! 'This night your soul is required of you; and the things you have prepared, whose will they be?' So is he who lays up treasure for himself, and is not reach toward God." "Take heed, and beware of all covetousness; for a man's life does not consist in the abundance of his possessions"

How could any level-headed leader, who is aware of the havocs caused by the first and second world wars, be consciously paving way for a third under the camouflage of acting for the interest of the Russian-speaking majority in Crimea. Should nations interfere with the affairs of another simply because it speaks the same language with part of it and militarily stronger? How could one, for a show of power, instigate, insinuate and arouse racism in the consciousness of an independent sovereign nation regardless of a calculated eventual disruption of world peace. The ruthlessness of such a leap portrays Putin a threat to world peace, provoking in defiance to the opinion of the rest of the world, in his selfish ambition impair diplomatic negotiations from America and Europe. The assumption the deposed Ukrainian leader sought assistance from him sounds like a germinated seed in due season to serve the purpose of the secret yearning of a man whose political ambition is to him more important than life itself, so much so, the scare of perdition has no effect on him. Had this been the contrary, he would otherwise have left Ukraine, as did the rest of the world, to solve their problems themselves, which indeed they almost achieved, had it not been for the unpatriotic president, a stooge of Russia, who sold the peace of his country for power in this transistory world at the risk of perdition.

>Hear o you in love with yourself, with this world,
>Transient is the fate of this world, all her Pomp,
>In no distant time shall be no more, all gone,
>Gone things so much your fancy did capture, And
>You o lover of self also gone to be no more.
>
>No more to be in this world of your obsession,
>To a world unknown, the abode of Satan prince
>of hell, author of wickedness and Pomp of this
>transient world. O lover of self and Pomp of this
>world, consider life with Satan, the devil, in hell.
>
>Yet Time, precious Time you do have, but not long,
>Hearken to the Voice of God, open your heart as
>He stands at the door and knocks, while you can.
>Accept God's love in Jesus Christ Your worthy
>Redeemer, gain life not death, flee the pit of hell.
>
>O you in love with yourself, with this world, despite your resistance, the Sacred Heart of Jesus aches for you, embrace love which you desperately seek. Poor Lover of self, do you not know Jesus is Love? Everything is His, the Lord of Heaven and Earth. O how desperately He awaits your 'yes' to give you Heaven.

My heart is filled with great sorrow as I contemplate the agony in the most Sacred Heart of Jesus over the many reprobates, souls who would end up, on their own free-will, in perdition. Do you not realize the Almighty Father is the most loving of Fathers, the best Father, that His Heart is troubled, yearning for the hearts of His children whom He infinitely loves. Jesus's Heart is desperately longing for you to give Him your heart, to reciprocate His love. He wants to take care of your heart, fill you with so much love, so you can understand the meaning of love and rest your search, as you would embrace peace. The God Who so richly loves you, so infinitely so as to take flesh, without counting the cost, to be like you, went through the subsequent terrible torture, all the humiliation, even the torturous death on the cross for love of you, how else do you want this wonderful God Who is love to prove His love for you?

What stops you from believing in His existence? Did He not endow you with intellect, with reason to find Him in His creation? Why hurt such a sweet God Who desires nothing but your happiness? After all, He is the Author and Giver of life, the Creator of all that is, seen and unseen, yet He is pleading with you to repent and turn away from sin, from your evil ways so you can have life abundantly. Remember He created you and has every right over you, yet He pleads with you to return to Him for your Eternal happiness. It is of no advantage to willfully offend the Almighty God Who in His infinite Goodness calls you His child and gave you His Heart. Therefore, for the benefit of your soul, would it not be wise you took good care of God's Heart and put a deaf ear to the enticement of Satan, the father of liars, while relying on the Grace and Mercy of God for a way of escape from the entanglement in sin, because He would never permit the enemy to tempt you above that which you are able.

Nevertheless, the tune to which the world today is dancing, creates the impression society is intentionally offending God, daring to see what

He would do. Having polluted the world with moral decay, sexual laxity, abortion, euthanasia, same-sex marriage and so on, which has become a thorn in the flesh to every level-headed human being who has affinity to God. Society aids the enemy, Satan, in so doing, to destroy humanity. Do those in society who indulge in such mortal sins not realize they are executioners of our Lord Jesus Christ of the present day. They crucify our good Lord each time they indulge in such deadly sins. How appalling, shameless and daring todays fashion has become. Society has lost the touch of modesty to embrace sexual allure in her fashion, the enemy's weapon to destroy the temple of God, the body of man. This absurdity has reached its peak, so much so, that it is manifested in the manner most female moderators in the media decorate themselves in such fashions that denote the tendency to advertise self as an object of lust. One cannot fail to observe RTL television Deutschland seems to be wanting in modest dressing. Do you not realize the exposure of one's body is disgracing Jesus? Yes, it is Jesus being exposed. Do you not realize He was three times stripped? At the scourging, when He was mocked and crowned with thorns and during the crucifixion? You may or may not be Christian, hopefully you value your soul and would want to spend Eternity with Jesus eternally in Heaven and not with Satan in hell which is the second death. Perhaps, you did not realize indecent dressing is a disgrace to Jesus but now you know, therefore, it is high time you did something to it for your salvation.

"You have heard that it was said, ' you shall not commit adultery.' But I say to you that everyone who looks at a woman lustfully has already committed adultery with her in his heart" Matt. 5 vs 25 – 28 Jesus said. Why then be a source for your brother to stumble with indecent clothing? Do you not think you have a share in his guilt? Therefore, "If your right eye causes you to sin, pluck it out and throw it away; it is better that you lose one of your members than that your whole body be thrown into hell" Matt. 5 vs 29.

Unfortunately, some Christian women also indulge in such practices without realizing how deeply they hurt Jesus. Simply because they want to be in tune with fashion, they forget the writing of St Paul "... do not be in conformity with the world." Moreover, it is astonishing seeing some women attend mass in transparent clothes, mini gowns, hot pants, exposure of breasts in deep cut blouses, in skirts cut through to expose the thighs. One tends to forget the House of God is a House of prayer, for adoration and worship, therefore, the center of attraction is the Almighty God, no one has the right to draw the attention of the congregation to herself or to himself with indecent clothing. Men are not exempted, though this is rampant with women. This is sinful. It shows no respect to Jesus. It is an affront to dare receive Him, the Almighty God in the Sacrament of His Love in such indecent clothes. Jesus is being hurt. He is being tied up in the hearts of such people and scourged.

The question arises whether the priests do not see them, if they do, what stops them from warning such women either personally or in their Homilies. Again one wonders why we cannot warn each other against such ill behavior which hurts our Lord, after all are we not one big family of God, brothers and sisters of Jesus Christ? Has Jesus not suffered enough? To have our good Lord nourish our souls with himself in the Eucharist is a wonderful gift of Love to be received in awe and with humility, after self-examination, being sure one is in a state of Grace. It should not be a routine but to be received with love in total obedience to the rules of our Catholic Faith for receiving our Lord. A regular reception of the Sacrament of Reconciliation, once a month or at least four times in the year makes such a situation avoidable. This helps one be more aware of who one is, a child of the Almighty God, and helps one grow in loving God. One should not make sin a habit, sinning with the notion to go afterwards to confession. One should always bear on mind, it is the Almighty God in His Supreme Being, the Holy Trinity, truly present in the Eucharist, Who can neither deceive nor be deceived, therefore approach and receive in awe and in humble gratitude. Let us marvel at the greatness and power of God to conceal His Greatness and Beauty in the Host, a piece of bread, for the nourishment of the soul, to prepare the soul to share His Divine life with Him. Wonder, ponder, admire and love the God of love Who created all things with love and for love.

How wonderful it is that God, despite our shortcomings invites us to abundant life. Unfortunately, rather than see the genuineness of God's invitation and love He is often misunderstood. God hates sin, humanity, saturated with sin, needs to be purified like gold, to be worthy of God's love. The Most Precious Blood of Jesus Christ, the price of our redemption, from the original sin, inherited from Adam and Eve, reunited man with God, with the Eternal Father. Through baptism the original sin is forgiven and forgotten. But there is still the need for individual struggle to eradicate the effect of sin, the desire for sin, to allow oneself to be transformed by God so as to resemble God Who made him, in His image, with whom he is to spend eternity eternally. To this end, therefore, God permits evil but He does not cause evil, for the good of man. Yes, God does allow suffering, after all He had the worst of it, for the maturity of the soul in the growth of virtues for a share in His Divine life and also for the salvation of souls incapable of carrying their crosses. God's invitation to abundant life, a share in His Divine life, a loving inheritance for humanity from the Eternal Father, is for everyone, but the only obstacle is indulgence in sin, a „NO" to God's love.

"Ho, everyone who thirsts, come to the waters; and he who has no money, come, buy and eat! Come, buy wine and milk without money and without price. Why do you spend your money for that which is not bread, and your labor for that which does not satisfy? Hearken diligently to me, and eat what is good, and delight yourselves in fatness. Incline your ear, and come to me; hear, that your soul may live; and I will make with you an everlasting covenant, my steadfast, sure love for David......For as the rain and the snow come down from heaven, and return not thither but water the earth, making it bring forth and sprout, giving seed to the sower and bread to the eater, so shall my word be that goes forth from my mouth; it shall not return to me empty, but it shall accomplish that which I purpose, and prosper in the thing for which I sent it"

What can surpass the love of God, Nothing!
Beautiful delicious, pure holy sweet Love.
Fortunate is he who finds this beautiful love.
Faithful, dependable, generous, fulfilling love.
Sweet taste, minute though it be, of the great
Heavenly Bliss for souls faithful to God's Love.

O this soul of mine fortunate thou be, pierced
with the arrows of Divine Love. You melt in the
Flavor of Love so sweet, engulfed in the sweet
caresses of Beloved so Divine, consumed by
Flames of Love so utterly sweet, so Divine.

My Heart in contemplation sweet, united with the
Sacred Heart of Jesus my Beloved so sweet, so
dear, the gentle breeze, His Breath, gently my forehead caressing, His sweet voice softly, tenderly,
assuringly, whispering His sweet love for me, His
sweet Cinderella Beloved dear of His Sacred Heart.

Deep in admiration of nature so sweetly beautiful,
With lingering eyes beholding the wonderful Creation
Of my Beloved, my Hero, the love of my life so sweet,
O what delight to my soul, as my Beloved a kiss on
My lips passionately places saying I made it all for you.

"For God alone my soul waits in silence; from him comes my salvation. He only is my rock and my salvation, my fortress; I shall not be greatly moved. How long will you set upon a man to shatter him, all of you, like a leaning wall, a tottering fence? ...Trust in him at all times, O people; pour out your heart before him; God is a refuge for us. Ps. 62 vs 2 – 3, 8 – 9.

"Worthy art thou, our Lord and God, to receive glory and honor and power; for thou didst create all things, and by thy will they existed and were created" Rev. 4 vs 11.

For Your wonderful beautiful creation O great good God of Beauty, bountiful in mercy, all glory and honor be yours forever – Amen.

– End –